ADVANCE PRAISE

"Who knew I could fall in love wit[   ]ob
Osterlund did, that's who. And in *H*[   ]ve
with them—and her—too, in this moving and fascinating book about
birds, loss, and finding a true home in the world."
> —CHERYL STRAYED, author of #1 *New York Times* bestseller
> *Wild: Lost and Found on the Pacific Crest Trail*

"*Holy Mōlī* is a labor of love. The love of magic. The magic of hope. And
that's just the book. Just wait till you meet the birds and the people whose
faith tends them. A million years in the making, this is a story of a re-
kindling of Life's most blessedly fierce and fiercely sacred flame: return.
Renewal. No better tale exists. Lesser tales need not apply."
> —CARL SAFINA, author of *Eye of the Albatross: Visions of Hope and Survival*
> and *Beyond Words: What Animals Think and Feel*

"I read *Holy Mōlī* with mounting amazement. It's wonderfully informa-
tive; Hob Osterlund also knows the albatross in the deepest sense, beyond
science. It's written with wit and humor and passion and love and pain.
It's lively and vibrant and vigorous. It's imaginative and speculative and
shimmering with implication and intimation. You cannot help but turn
the page, which is a delicious thing to say of any book. It's about a riveting
creature unlike any other in the world and perhaps the universe. It's about
reverence and respect and resurrection. Quietly and shyly it's also about the
author, which is how books in which the author appears ought to be and
hardly ever are. It's a remarkable book that I still think about a lot long
after I finished reading it, which seems to me the sign of a Very Fine Book
Indeed. I hang that sign on this book with confidence and something very
much like awe."
> —BRIAN DOYLE, author of *The Plover* and *Mink River*

"The Gulf Coast artist, Walt Anderson, calls birds 'holes in heaven through
which a man or woman may pass.' The New Mexican sage, Martín Prechtel,
calls them 'an almost molecular presence in our psyches and souls.' In the
spirit of these seers, an orphan named Hob set forth with indefatigable wit,
curiosity, eloquence, and a camera named for her departed mom, made a
dual home for herself both on the north shore of Kaua'i and smack dab in

the heart of Jesus' adage Consider the fowls of the air, and the very skies have been served by the interspecies communion that has resulted. *Holy Mōlī* is a healing; a hoot; a transmission of gravity-defying wonder."

— DAVID JAMES DUNCAN, author of *The River Why* and *The Brothers K*

"It is an act of profound courage for any human being to decide, in these environmentally cataclysmic times, to love a wild thing completely. Hob Osterlund was put on earth to bear witness to the Kaua'i Mōlī; and in telling that story, reconnect us to our own."

— PAM HOUSTON, author of *Contents May Have Shifted*

"*Holy Mōlī* is a remarkable story of observation and healing, of loss and adaptation, of curiosity and wisdom. From the early death of her mother to her present-day role as citizen scientist, Hob Osterlund takes us on fascinating journeys into her family's past and the daily life of albatross colonies on Kaua'i. Her affection for these extraordinary birds makes this book a winner. I loved every page."

— HOPE EDELMAN, author of *Motherless Daughters*

"Hob Osterlund is a wonderful writer—intelligent, powerful, full of grace and humor—and she has a wonderful story to tell. Who else could so perfectly describe the sweet smell of an albatross feather or the swelling in her heart when a chick she's known since the moment of hatch finally takes wing?"

— KATHLEEN DEAN MOORE, author of *Wild Comfort: The Solace of Nature*

"*Holy Mōlī* flows with a funny, lively, unique style—lots of snazzy and jazzy writing, sparkling language, and delightful, entertaining turns of thought. It glitters with a strong, humorous voice."

— SHARMAN APT RUSSELL, author of *Diary of a Citizen Scientist: Chasing Tiger Beetles and Other New Ways of Engaging the World*

"Hob is one helluva writer and *Holy Mōlī* is holy-crap good. Lyrical, uplifting, heart-breaking, sweet, and a whole lot else."

— SCOTT WEIDENSAUL, Pulitzer Prize finalist for *Living on the Wind: Across the Hemisphere With Migratory Birds*

"*Holy Mōlī* touches a deep chord that reverberates in all our hearts. Wondrous mysteries of life and death and nature and the webs of interconnections. Hob Osterlund's journey of healing leads to an incredible gift for all of us; her wise and witty words and exquisite images wake us up to the world of one of the most amazing creatures on this planet, the albatross. So grateful for Hob's teachings that encourage us to really see and soar."
—SUSAN BAUER-WU, author of *Leaves Falling Gently* and
President of Mind & Life Institute

"Hob Osterlund is a witness to beauty. Her words ground that sacred witnessing on the page with joyous revelations, not without sorrow. The full range of emotion is hers. I look forward to her ongoing relationship of wonder with the albatross."
—TERRY TEMPEST WILLIAMS, author of
Refuge: An Unnatural History of Family and Place

"*Holy Mōlī* will grab the heart and imagination of everybody and their mother. Not only is the story at once both simple and epic, but Hob Osterlund—with her generous spirit, her brilliant storytelling, her uniquely qualified perspective and her unflappable charm—will win her an audience who will find nourishment, joy, solace, and inspiration in her writing."
—GINA BARRECA, author of
They Used to Call Me Snow White But I Drifted

"The albatross is a bird of superlatives, and Hob Osterlund is a superlative writer extraordinarily devoted to her magnificent subject. She's adept at capturing the bird's divine grace and endearing awkwardness, relaying the drama and humor of its days, and inspiring her readers to protect this legendary wanderer. You'll love *Holy Mōlī*!"
—SY MONTGOMERY, author of *Birdology*

"I love Hob's writing. Her stories are delightful, entertaining and intimate. Because of her rare ability to take us inside the lives of these amazing birds, the albatross may fly onto center stage among charismatic animals, just as penguins did a few years ago."
—STACEY O'BRIEN, author of *New York Times* bestseller
Wesley the Owl: The Remarkable Love Story of an Owl and His Girl

Holy Mōlī

Holy Mōlī

Albatross and Other Ancestors

HOB OSTERLUND

Oregon State University Press　　Corvallis

All photographs by Hob Osterlund

Library of Congress Cataloging-in-Publication Data

Names: Osterlund, Hob.
Title: Holy mōlī : albatross and other ancestors / Hob Osterlund.
Description: Corvallis : Oregon State University Press, [2016] | Includes
  bibliographical references.
Identifiers: LCCN 2015051037 (print) | LCCN 2016009348 (ebook) | ISBN
  9780870718489 (original trade pbk. : alk. paper) | ISBN 9780870718496
  (ebook)
Subjects: LCSH: Albatrosses—Hawaii. | Laysan albatross—Hawaii.
Classification: LCC QL696.P63 O88 2016 (print) | LCC QL696.P63
  (ebook) | DDC
  598.4/2—dc23
LC record available at http://lccn.loc.gov/201505103

♾ This paper meets the requirements of ANSI/NISO Z39.48-1992
(Permanence of Paper).

Oregon State University Press
121 The Valley Library
Corvallis OR 97331-4501
541-737-3166 • fax 541-737-3170
www.osupress.oregonstate.edu

to Joanne

Genealogy

MATRILINEAL LINES

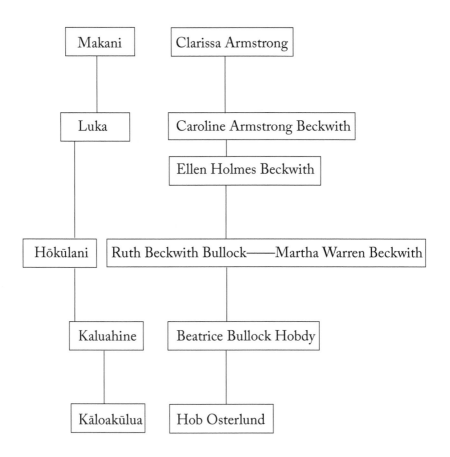

Makani	Clarissa Armstrong
Luka	Caroline Armstrong Beckwith
	Ellen Holmes Beckwith
Hōkūlani	Ruth Beckwith Bullock——Martha Warren Beckwith
Kaluahine	Beatrice Bullock Hobdy
Kāloakūlua	Hob Osterlund

Contents

One

Arriving

Albatross courtship

I sat cross-legged in a grove of ironwood trees on the north shore of Kaua'i. The ground was spongy with years of fallen needles, ruddy as the dirt. Wispy branches rippled in the gentle trade winds. Sounds of the forest swirled like smoke: the surge of the surf below, the trill of songbirds, the balmy breeze. It smelled like rain.

A party was rocking on the plateau above me. One by one, adolescent Laysan albatross—known as *mōlī* in Hawaiian—were arriving from their rounds of other coastal colonies. All of them were crazy for courtship. They stood on tiptoes, pointed their bills skyward, and made music in the manner of their clan everywhere. Some notes were high-pitched like children screeching with joy in the waves of Hanalei Bay, some were low and plaintive like monks chanting Buddhist mantras. The birds bobbed themselves into oblivion, lost as dervishes in the dance.

Prior to my having the opportunity to monitor these magnificent beings, most of my knowledge about birds came from three sources: my nature-loving mother, the pigeons I raised as a young girl, and my undergraduate studies in ecology at Cal Berkeley. My awareness of albatross, however, was limited to the misleading metaphor from the eighteenth-century epic poem by Samuel Taylor Coleridge, *The Rime of the Ancient Mariner*. The familiar expression *albatross around your neck* connotes a heavy burden, an endless problem, an inescapable legacy.

It's a bad rap, and wholly undeserved. In *The Rime,* a benevolent albatross leads a marooned ship to safety, saving the lives of all the sailors on board. One of the mariners gets drunk and kills the mōlī with his crossbow. Just so, the wind perishes. In retaliation, the mariner's shipmates—all of them now dying of thirst—force the mariner to wear the bird's big body around his neck as a symbol of his ignorance.

In the centuries since, *The Rime*'s avian hero somehow morphed from innocent to guilty in the collective human imagination. It's a good act, but nothing could be further from the truth. No matter what measure you use, mōlī characteristics are superlative. They live longer in the wild than most—if not all—feathered species. The current title "oldest known wild bird in the world" is held by Wisdom, a sixty-four-year-old who still raises babies and appears forever young, indistinguishable from birds six decades her junior. Albatross are peerless parents. Mothers and fathers work equally hard at the rigors of rearing a chick. Laysans fly the equivalent of New York to San Francisco *round trip* just to deliver dinner to their chicks. Adults forage millions of square miles of the North Pacific, from British Columbia to Japan, then somehow manage to find their postage-stamp-sized nesting grounds without the help of a single landmark. Hawaiian colonies have a significant presence of female-female pairs, a phenomenon not well known in other nonhuman animals. As a rule, albatross are peace loving. They wouldn't recognize a predator if it walked up and bit them on their bills. In Hawai'i they are considered *'aumākua*, cherished ancestors and guardian spirits.

As impressive as Wisdom is, there's at least one other notable pioneer, a bird we'll call Makani. Although albatross typically practice extraordinary fidelity to their hatch sites, our hero chose another option. She flew south to Kaua'i, an island where her species had likely been extirpated a millennium before. Like the vast majority of Laysans, she grew up on Midway Atoll. Why did she bypass such an enormous pool of potential mates and travel more than one thousand miles in the opposite direction of her family and primary food source? Why did she leave her home and risk the dangers of an island with a sizable census of humans?

Makani ultimately found a mate, brought him home, and raised a baby. All the hundreds of chicks hatched on Kaua'i since 1979 owe her a debt of gratitude, as do all future generations. They fly on the wings of her courage and wayfinding.

I squinted through my telephoto to freeze-frame the mōlī singles bar scene above me. The birds used more than a dozen dance steps, synchronizing moves like the bow, the stare, and the whinny. There was the head flick, the bill clapper, and the sky snap. The bill-under-wing posture resembled Kevin Kline's armpit sniff in *A Fish Called Wanda*. The rapid bill touching looked like Olympic fencing parries, and the mutual moo seemed frankly ecstatic. Collectively the movements appeared to be a creative dance depiction of an entire albatross lifespan, a collage of positions of nest building, food begging, flight takeoffs, walking, napping, and lovemaking. It was all there, their story, a living ritual and a rowdy celebration.

With wingspans as wide as Kobe Bryant is tall, you'd think the birds would be hefty. Not at all. The basketball player's body is about thirty times heavier than theirs. Partly constructed with air sacs, their structure is supported by a skeleton of hollow bones. Imagine an inflated football. Cover it with feathers, white on the torso and dark chocolate on the wings, then add wide webbed feet. Put on a head with intelligent dark eyes. Add a pinkish bill with a sharp grey tip that can tickle or tear flesh, depending. Add more feathered footballs with their groove on, and you've got yourself a bash.

I was so focused on the party I didn't notice an animal coming up behind me until it was too late. I turned my head, my heart in my throat. There was no need for fear. It was an albatross headed up the hill. Her webs were as supple as goatskin gloves. Her footsteps created an almost inaudible crunch in the ironwood litter, like the sound of your fingertips on your scalp when you run your hand through your hair.

"Hey," I whispered gratefully, my anxiety dissipating. The bird gave no indication she shared either my fright or my relief. In fact, she took no notice of me at all. Since mōlī usually nest on uninhabited Hawaiian Islands with no native predators, most of them haven't learned to regard humans with any particular alarm. This albatross only had eyes for the boogie on the bluff. She stepped on my foot as she padded past. I was as irrelevant as a root.

I'd never received higher praise.

How could that be? For most of my life, beneath the surface current of my days, I'd felt an undertow of shame. I'd felt dangerous—criminal even—since the death of my mother when I was a child. It was such a horrific loss I could only assume it was my fault. I had no other framework to hang it from. No one suggested I had caused my mother's illness, but I inferred it all the same. In a way, the absence of blame from others made my offense seem all the more heinous. Whatever I'd done must have been so awful, I told myself, no one could say it aloud. It was up to me to name it, to risk its poison on my tongue. I had vowed to bring my mother back, to reverse the damage I'd done, whatever it took.

Immediately after the albatross stepped on my foot, I was washed with a mysterious and glorious sensation of freedom. It took a long time to find words to describe it, but it felt like the bird had somehow offered me a brief pardon from my crime. If such an iconic animal reckoned me as benign as a stump, perhaps it was possible to be released from the prison of my own promise to my mother.

I didn't know it then, but my resolve to serve the birds began in that moment.

Over the years, I evolved from being an admirer with a schoolgirl crush to a citizen scientist with a camera and a team. Because of the birds' urgent need for safe nesting in places well above sea level, I founded the Kaua'i Albatross Network and became a habitat liaison for several private property owners. I documented leg bands, trapped predators, assisted with egg adoptions, found funding sources, coordinated a live-streaming camera, served on a task force for an ordinance to control feral cats, and gathered with experts on mongoose eradication. I took tens of thousands of photos with my camera, "Beatrice," named after my mother. I guided visitors, published articles, and gave community talks.

No creature—winged, furred, or high-heeled—is more stunning or entertaining to me. From a distance, an albatross in flight glows like an orb; banking perpendicular to the earth, the bird's profile looks like a flying fettuccine. Close up, charcoal eye shadows draw you into a mesmerizing face. It's the stuff of awe and poetry.

In the last century we've given them countless opportunities to distrust us. We've killed inconceivable numbers of them for their feathers.

We've bombed their nurseries. We've stolen mountains of their eggs for albumen. Still, they don't look at us and see an enemy. How can that be?

There are other questions. Was the Kaua'i appearance of mōlī merely coincidence, a statistical artifact, a random meaningless act? Or did the birds sense something looming at Midway—their low-lying mother ship—the largest albatross colony on earth and home to more than 95 percent of their species? We know they can predict weather. Can they predict sea level rise? Are they building their Noah's Ark?

I got to albatross by way of a mysterious visitation. In the winter of 1979, the cultural anthropologist Martha Warren Beckwith—my grandmother's cousin—appeared in my dream. I don't recall her speaking a single word. She simply handed me her book, *Hawaiian Mythology*. Although I hadn't seen her since I was ten years old, it took only those brief moments for Auntie Martha to launch me on a new trajectory. I awakened with a powerful pull to the islands. I admit I fought it. I questioned its authenticity. I tried to forget it. I blamed it on bad homemade wine. Ultimately, I considered moving only because I needed some distance from a failed relationship. I found families for my dogs, quit my job, and boarded a plane to Honolulu. Although Hawai'i was home to several generations of my ancestors, I didn't know anyone who still lived there. I had a few hundred dollars in my pocket. No one understood why I had to move thousands of miles away, not even me.

Martha Warren Beckwith, circa 1916

Several events happened within a span of a few months of my relocation in 1979. Makani's daughter Luka flew, the first chick to fledge from Kaua'i in perhaps a thousand years. I happened upon a few albatross courting, discovered a profound kinship, and learned mōlī was their Hawaiian name. I read *Hawaiian Mythology* and was exposed to the concept of 'aumākua, or guardian ancestors in animal form. These events occurred in such a close cluster, it was as if they were part of a benevolent puzzle eager to reveal itself. It would take another twenty-five years and two Himalayan journeys for the larger picture to come into focus.

In 2001, a group of friends and I decided to travel to the remote country of Bhutan. Central to our itinerary was a trek to higher altitudes, to the mountain home of yak herders and yeti sightings. Two long flights got us to Kolkata, India, and a shorter one got us to Paro, home of Bhutan's only international airport. Once we got settled in the land known as the "Forbidden Kingdom," we visited monasteries and took day hikes until we were acclimated to the base elevation of seventy-three hundred feet. Gathering for dinner at our lodgings, we were eager to start the trek the next morning.

It was early in the visitor season, so we had the hotel almost to ourselves. We barely noticed when two other guests, both western men, took seats in the dining room. At some point one of them approached our table. "I don't want to ruin your fun," he said. Maybe he chose to address me because he saw wrapped gifts in front of me. "What's up?" I asked, offering him a piece of birthday cake.

"We just heard someone set off a bomb in New York this morning," he said. "We don't know how bad it was." We thanked him for letting us know. In those days newspapers were delivered via India, and were a few days behind. Television reception was skeletal. Facebook, Twitter, and Instagram had not been invented. We could not send or receive e-mails. There was no cell phone coverage. Connections, even from hotel ground lines, were unreliable. We went to bed without further information.

As we started our trek early the next morning, several apple-cheeked children followed us. They were excited to practice their English skills and charmed us with their inquiries. One boy said "Madam, which country?" Another asked "Where you going, madam?"

One shy girl, covering her mouth with her hand, asked me "Madam, you have issues?"

How, I wondered, could I even begin to answer that question? Smiling, I opted for the easiest reply. "No I don't," I said. The girl's face saddened. She paused to consider her reply.

"Madam, you are spinster, isn't it?"

She hadn't intended to be funny, but she succeeded anyway—in part because she was right. I had no children, was fifty-three and unmarried. Even if we had a language in common, it was clearly not an opportune time to sit down and discuss the concept of *partner* with my young friend. I squatted in front of her and put my hand on her shoulder. "You are all my children," I said. She beamed.

After we learned their names, we asked why they were out of school on a weekday. Namgay had the answer. "Because two big buildings in America fell down, isn't it." The date was September 12, 2001. His Majesty Jigme Singye Wangchuck, the Fourth Druk Gyalpo and beloved king, had closed all government offices and schools so people could light butter lamps to pray for the United States. Even when we learned the "two big buildings in America" were the Twin Towers, there was nothing we could do but continue on our way into the mountains. We may have been among the few westerners in the world to miss the barrage of wrenching images over the next several days. Hiking uphill at altitude has a way of minimizing conversation, so we each digested the news in our own quiet way.

Over the following weeks, in the dark maelstrom of grief and rage related to the attacks on the World Trade Center, I regularly asked myself how I could personally contribute to a saner world. In those contemplations, one sentence kept coming back to me. *The king closed the government so they could pray for us.* If our planet stood a chance, surely it would be because of behaviors like His Majesty's. Not many Americans knew much about Bhutan in those days, although the royal family's concept of Gross National Happiness was starting to get coverage. Word was also getting out about Bhutan's unprecedented environmental policies. I wanted to share the story of a benevolent Buddhist monarch and how he responded to a global tragedy. We desperately need to know there are people like him, I thought, to know it's possible for leaders to act compassionately. Not just toward its own citizens or toward citizens in countries with diplomatic ties, but toward life.

Back home in Hawai'i I started giving presentations about Bhutan. I carried photos with me and talked about the kingdom with anyone who would listen. I published a piece in what was then the *Honolulu Advertiser*. Then, in 2004, I got a chance to return to the Himalayas. On that visit I got a surprising and unlikely opportunity to interview Her Royal Highness Ashi Dorji Wangmo Wangchuck, Queen of Bhutan (now Queen Mother.) Her Majesty had trekked the far corners of her country—places inaccessible to motorized vehicles—and returned ever more devoted to the welfare of her people. Brilliant, beautiful, and soft-spoken, she was not interested in talking about herself; instead, she wanted to promote the good works of the Tarayana Foundation, a nonprofit organization she founded. I later wrote up that interview for a Hawai'i magazine.

Her Majesty Ashi Dorji Wangmo Wangchuck with the author

Who knew that story would lead me to the albatross on Kaua'i? When a mutual friend saw the article, he encouraged me to meet Patricia. Patricia and her husband Joseph had recently helped to install solar power in a Bhutanese village. They invited me for a visit at their home, which happened to be only fifteen miles from my own. It was only a matter of days before I found myself sitting on their lanai, sipping tea and swapping stories. Sometime in that conversation, Joseph casually told me they had albatross nesting on their land. "Come see them anytime," he said. At that point I knew enough about the birds to be excited about the offer, but I didn't have the foggiest notion where it would lead.

It was almost the end of the 2003–2004 nesting season when Joseph led me up a path to the bluff on his property and pointed toward the birds.

"Stay as long you like," he said and disappeared into the woods. About one hundred feet back from the edge of the cliff was an abandoned nest built of mounded ironwood needles, so I decided to sit in it, to make it my observation post. It conformed to me as easily as warm sand. Beneath me in the concavity were other occupants—black, shiny objects that I later learned were regurgitated squid beaks—too sharp for the previous tenant to safely digest.

Trade winds cooled the summer sun. Branches waved overhead, mottling the ground and quieting my mental chatter. A western meadowlark commended the view from the highest tree. Turquoise waves pounded ancient lava rocks below, potholing and polishing them. In the colony were several 'tross chicks, almost ready to fledge. They showed no interest in me. At five months old, they looked like goofy characters made up of two creatures. From the neck down they were mature adults. From the neck up they were furry, their heads covered with wooly brown babushkas. One bird stood near the drop-off. Since she hatched, it appeared she had built four new nests for herself, each one marching closer to the ledge than the last, like elephant footprints.

Before her, the sea, the unknown, full of risks and grand possibilities.

Behind her, the earth, the familiar, full of risks. Zero possibilities.

She would have to fly very soon if she was going to stay alive.

She flapped her wings and hopped in place. She cocked her head like a puppy, curious, full of questions. Did she get a reply? She tilted her head, opened her bill and swallowed the sky. With that she released every prayer, punch line and curse, every poem, chant and giggle, every plea, wail and hosanna; in short and in the highest, all that could possibly be said forevermore—with a moo.

Laysan albatross lived in Hawai'i long before we walked the earth. Kaua'i, the first of the main islands to burst steaming from the Pacific, may have hosted the birds' earliest colonies. Millions of years later, after the arrival of people and predators, the colonies likely disappeared. But the great creatures could still be seen at sea, gliding on gravity and wind, as if the elements were amusement rides designed for their pleasure.

In the mid-1970s a few mōlī were spotted on the bluffs above the beaches of Kaua'i. Because there was no protection from domestic dogs and wild pigs, their early attempts at breeding failed. All that changed in 1979, when Makani's chick fledged from a northern part of the island.

Makani's first home was very different from Kaua'i. She grew up among hundreds of thousands of chicks on Midway Atoll. Crowds were central to the fabric of her life, a familiar mix of flirtations and territorial disputes, preens and regurgitations, squeals of indignation and murmurs of affection. Midway may be part of the northwestern Hawaiian Islands, but it's not exactly tropical. It sits on the same latitude as Thimphu, the capital of Bhutan. In the winter, daytime temperatures can vary as much as thirty degrees. One minute it's warm like the jungle, the next minute it's cold like the mountains. Squalls come and go like marching bands, all percussion and brass, bussed in from the north by massive purple clouds that ride the wild northern horizon. There is no end to the wind. There is no beginning, no middle. There are no boundaries, no owners, no opposing teams, no speed limits. There is always the wind, since before islands were islands, since before dinosaurs gave birds the gift of flight.

Makani had skillful parents who were adept at delivering dinner. When she was a few months old, she sported a downy Mohawk and was almost ready to fly for the first time. She knew nothing of her destiny; she knew only hunger. Hunger for food, for weightlessness, for merging with the sky. The smells of the sea were overwhelmingly seductive to her. She picked up twigs and leaves from the ground, as if collecting small bits of courage.

In rehearsal for her maiden voyage, Makani jumped here and there, sideways and forward. At first she got only a few seconds of air. The more she practiced, the more lift she got. When the marching band charged in with a drum corps of pounding rain, Makani took a bigger risk. She leapt as high as she could, gained a little yardage, and did a face plant. She was not discouraged. She kept going, jumping on a trampoline of grass and sand, up and down on her toes, peeping, her wings outstretched. She bounced across the asphalt runway until solid ground reached an abrupt end. She splashed into the ocean and bobbed with a flotilla of hundreds of her fellow fledglings. She rested for a few minutes to get her bearings, gazing up at a cluster of great frigate birds, the ʻiwa, cruising like airborne Cadillac coupes.

She didn't notice the dark shadows lurking beneath her. Suddenly one of her fellow fledglings disappeared in a terrifying commotion of white water and shark teeth. Talk about incentive. Makani ran on the surface, webs slapping water, never sinking, a Jesus bird, flapping with all her might until she got liftoff. *Hana hou!* Encore! She was really and truly the pilot of her own craft. Makani followed her nose, using wind and gravity to propel her forward. She had to teach herself to forage for food, and over the weeks and months she got good at it. Wherever she went, she flew solo. For years she explored an enormous region of the North Pacific, from Japan to the Aleutian Islands to British Columbia, landing only on the surface of the sea. She forgot what land felt like.

Her to-do list was deceptively short: *Fly far. Find squid.*

Then, when she was four years old, two more items were added. *Go home. Find love.*

Makani obeyed. Birds from every species of albatross are as faithful as the stars. They almost never relocate to a distant island devoid of colonies. It's so rare that a new location *might* occur on the globe once every hundreds of years, even longer. Oh sure, a bird from one island might pick a mate from a nearby island and go home with his new love. It happens. But to establish a whole new colony a thousand miles away? Where mates hook up, where chicks hatch and fledge and return to court? Never happens.

Well, almost never.

Makani felt an irresistible urge. She headed south from the Bering Sea and back toward home. When she got to Midway, something mysterious and miraculous happened. She overrode her own navigational commands. Why did she bypass her parents and a huge pool of potential partners? She had never before flown south of Midway. She crossed the twenty-eighth parallel. She kept going. And going. For thirteen hundred miles she flew in the opposite direction of her family and her primary food source. When she saw Kaua'i, she landed on a green hillside in an open field near a lighthouse. She stumbled. Her feet had not touched solid ground in four years. What drew her there? Albatross bones that predate the arrival of early Polynesians have been found in subfossil deposits on Kaua'i. Did Makani's prehistoric clan live on this very spot? Did she carry ancestral GPS in her cells?

Although Makani's arrival on Kaua'i was significant, it was not her meanest feat. What mattered was that she kept on returning. She managed to be okay without her family at Midway, without the crowds and the cacophony, without the marching bands and the temperature variations. She was somehow okay with mountains and bluffs and the strangely warm latitude. She was somehow okay with being a loner, though perhaps she later recruited a few of her Midway cohorts. She came back to Kaua'i year after year until she brought home her perfect mate. When she was nine years old, she made history by raising a healthy chick. The chick's name was Luka.

When Luka was ready to fly, she hopped up and down on the ground. She kept going, jumping on a trampoline of grass, her wings outstretched. She jumped into the arms of the wind and was carried out to sea. She knew exactly where she was. Because of Luka, a new colony was officially born unto the world. A colony from the land, the 'āina, the ancient island known as Kauaʻi. Like her mother before her, Luka had no concept of the vital role she would play for her species.

Just like Makani, all mated Laysan albatross spend several solo months at sea every year, from July to November. Then, from all over their range, they feel a pull as strong as the earth's own magnet. One by one, the birds switch their flight patterns from drift to dash, from cruise to clip. They are on a sudden mission, heading to their nesting grounds. It is baby-making time. As Sharman Apt Russell wrote in *Diary of a Citizen Scientist*, "The birth of the universe began with a bang, and the banging has never stopped."

No matter how many times I see an albatross land, I watch with admiration. It's not so much the physical act—though that too is a treat—but what the bird carries. A non-nester may take off and land a dozen times in several hours. That bird carries desire on one wing, pleasure on the other. A nester may be landing for the first time in two or three weeks. That bird carries a reflection of the open sea on its belly, a slice of sky on its back, and a chest full of love for its baby.

But a mate returning after an absence of many months? That bird is a living planetarium with starlight glittering on his head. That bird carries the North Pacific like a bride across a threshold, having touched her every surface with the gentle fingertips of a lover, riding her thrusting curves, never tiring of her arching pulsing power, exploring her rolling peaks and troughs, staring without fear into the eyes of her every storm and returning home like a binge drinker, ripped out of his gourd on the earth's magnetic field, his breath smelling of iron.

One season the first bird back was an especially handsome, vigorous male. He started nest construction within a few feet of his last year's spot. I watched him, hoping his ladylove would appear. But we both knew another possibility—she had probably perished. Their last season's chick died, malnutrition the likely culprit. It always takes two full-time parents to raise a hungry baby. If one goes missing, it's game over for their offspring. Could the mama not find sufficient squid? Did she drown after swallowing a piece of fish impaled with a hook on a long-line? Did she spiral from the sky in the middle of a wingbeat, her life force vanished?

I named their last year's chick Macaroon because she looked like she'd rolled in a vat of shredded coconut. With her punky white-tipped fluff, she was cute as claymation. Sadly, when all the other babes were fully feathered and ready to fly, Macaroon remained downy. I found her body face down one July afternoon, her wings spread wide, as if she had flown in her dreams.

But now it was another season, and her unattached papa was restless. He was ready to start a new family. He paced the colony. With feints, whinnies, and a puffed-up chest, he did his manly best to convince a few females they would not regret an intimate moment with him. His vibe earned him the name Randy.

Even though the girls reacted to Randy with sleepy stares and half-hearted rebukes, he stayed focused on his mission. One male snapped at him, warning him to back off. One bird did seem briefly interested, at least long enough for a short dance. When Randy was ready to get serious—about three minutes into the first and only date—he strutted like a drum major to his nest site. Something about the whole gig just wasn't working for her. She strolled away, stopping once or twice to glance over her shoulder.

Temporarily resigned to his solitude, Randy squatted in a shady grove of *Casuarina*. The ground was covered with a millennium's accumulation of volcanic soil, spongy with decades of needles from the trees. For me, walking in that forest was like walking on an old foam futon, ruddy with rain, sex, and guano. The sun made the ground smell sweet like summer; in monsoon, like wet feathers.

The *Casuarina* trees were immigrants to Hawai'i only a century before, but they practiced soil supremacy like they owned the place. Their chemical warfare prevented any plant—native or introduced—from growing beneath them. In this case, what was bad for native plants was good for native albatross. Incubating adults could get out of the sun, which was a blessed relief for birds accustomed to frigid storms. Parents could sculpt bowls from the branchlets. Week-old chicks—barely strong enough hold up their heads—could rearrange needles. Courting adults could toss them to the wind like golfers. Because of the soft ground, the birds could dance without interference from plants that could snag their webs, soft as kidskin.

More albatross arrived. Excited mates reunited after many months apart, preened and got down. After a couple of weeks, Randy seemed fully surrendered to his solitude. I thought he had returned to sea for the rest of the season, but a few days later he was back. If not for his leg band, I would never have known it was the same bird. He had found himself a new girl. Because she was banded on Oʻahu (likely at Kaʻena Point, the westernmost tip of the island), the home of 90 percent of Hawaiʻi's human population, she qualified as a Townie. To my knowledge she'd never before been a nester on Kauaʻi. Townie had become a Kauaʻi country girl, even though her GPS might have urged her to

Randy and Townie reunite after months of separation

another island one hundred miles away. Perhaps her commitment to Randy trumped her inner Garmin. Can you say *recalculating*?

In Townie's presence, Randy was transformed from horny to honey. I had never seen such a dramatic personality change without assistance from the pharmaceutical industry. Gone were his frenetic pleas. Gone was his urgency. He was all heart. He leaned into Townie, nuzzled her neck, squeaked sweet nothings. They stared into each other's eyes. They were a feathered version of two people lying on tussled silk sheets, spent and sweaty, illumined by candles and sharing a cigarette, listening to Amy Winehouse sing "Will You Still Love Me Tomorrow?"

There's an unmistakable serenity when the answer to the song's question is *Yes, I will love you tomorrow.*

Townie waited on the nest, her eyes half closed, feeling new life grow within her. Her egg would come soon. Randy did not leave her side. He was about to be a papa again. He wanted for nothing.

I was eager to visit the mother ship. Ever since my first glimpse of Laysan albatross decades before, I yearned to witness them in their wildest element, to see them by the millions in their ancestral homeland of Midway Atoll. The opportunity to visit Pihemanu—as it's known in Hawaiian—does not come around often. The refuge has been slimmed by several federal budget cuts; when the atoll was last open to research and ecotourism in 2012, only 330 people were given permits in the entire year. The following year even fewer were granted access.

In the fall of 2013, my first chance—perhaps my only chance—appeared. Invitations were sent to wait-listed candidates from Beth Flint of the US Fish and Wildlife Service. Our job would be to tally albatross nests. Beth kindly encouraged us to consider the physical and psychological rigors of the job before committing. We would work full-time for about three weeks, with days off only on Christmas and New Year's. We would be walking all day every day, except for when we were biking to our sectors or crawling under dense shrubs. When the wind kicked up, we would be retreating to open spaces to avoid getting smacked by falling limbs. We should be prepared for blazing sun, sudden squalls, and daytime temperatures that might vary as much as thirty degrees.

We would be carrying paint guns. Since each of us would pull the trigger thousands of times during the count, we should bring garden gloves and duct tape to prevent finger blisters. We would bushwhack through *Verbesina*—a noxious weed with nasty thorns—in thickets up to seven feet tall. We would traverse mine fields of petrel burrows; falling in them would be inevitable. We would live in barracks, sharing our rooms with commuting cockroaches and centipedes. Rust-colored water could rush from our faucets. Internet access would be intermittent and cell phone reception absent. We would be fed three meals a day, all with spicy Asian options, because half of the resident staff at Midway is from Thailand. We should buy flight insurance, or—if we'd rather take a pass—be prepared to personally pay thirty thousand dollars for an airlift should we require urgent medical attention. The Friends of Midway Association would help subsidize us; our out-of-pocket costs would be about two thousand dollars each, plus round-trip airfare from home to Honolulu.

My reply to the invitation, now that I had a detailed picture of the volunteer job?

I went weak in the knees just thinking about it.

I want to go to there.

Pihemanu is a minuscule speck of land in the North Pacific roughly halfway between the United States and Asia. A former military base and the site of an infamous World War II battle, the atoll consists of three islands: Sand, Eastern, and Spit. All are essentially flat and barely above sea level. The international dateline is only a few miles away. On a clear day—if you stand on the roof of the tallest building and train your binoculars westward—you can see tomorrow.

There's a lot of midway in Midway. It's in the Hawaiian archipelago, but not under the jurisdiction of the state of Hawai'i. It's in the same area code as Honolulu but not the same time zone. It has a modern runway but is not listed on a departures board anywhere in the world. It's a territory of the United States, but Americans need a passport and a special permit to visit.

When it was almost time to go, I packed my big blue duffel with an odd travel assortment. Rain pants, snorkel, fleece jacket, duct tape, secret Santa gift. I double-checked essentials for a remote outpost: cash, coffee, and corkscrew; Tilley hat, tick spray, and tripod. At the very last minute I stuffed in an absurd faux-zebra-skin shower cap—not for my hair, but for my bicycle seat. The bag bulged like a blimp.

When I finished scrubbing my boots clean of any possible hitch-hiking seeds, I drove to the Līhuʻe Airport for an easy thirty-minute flight to Honolulu. A cab whisked me to a small quiet lounge about two miles from the international terminal. Passengers with sturdy backpacks mingled; some wore camouflage, others were in uniform. Some were from the American mainland; some were Hawaiʻi residents. Most were women. All of us would soon board a chartered jet scheduled to fly some thirteen hundred miles northwest, the approximate equivalent of a journey from San Diego to Seattle. There were no tickets, no TSA, no public address announcements. Even before departure, the journey had elements of an odd hybrid between an espionage expedition and a luxury vacation. Or—you never know—maybe I had stumbled into the Narnia wardrobe.

The all-volunteer "survey team" boarded an eighteen-seat Gulfstream and was soon in the air above Waikiki, banking northwest toward Tokyo. When we got to a cruising altitude of forty-one thousand feet, we chased the sunset for nearly two hours. The horizon glowed with tangerine-tinted clouds until the Earth's rotation finally left us in the cosmic dust. The last sliver of the sun disappeared; night won.

The blue monitor displaying our progress was just above my left shoulder. Why are cartoon airplanes so riveting? A yellow line plotted our proximity to the international date line, with the home airport identified as the place of origin. Other than Honolulu, the entire North Pacific map showed only three cities worthy of highlighting.

Tokyo and Anchorage, those I got. But Magadan, a tiny Russian port? Go figure.

When we were thirty minutes away from our destination, the screen read *Altitude 41000 feet, Outside Temperature -70° F.* When we were ten minutes away, the cartoon plane hit the cartoon bull's-eye. *Midway Islands, 0 miles.*

Our descent was spooky. In order to prevent bird-aircraft collisions, landings always go down under the cover of darkness. There were no glowing lights on the wings, no lights on the landing strip. *Altitude 25 feet, Outside Temperature 69°.* We had no visual confirmation that terra firma was actually beneath our wings. My stomach dropped with the landing gear. Anxiety commandeered my brain and announced our imminent plunge into the Pacific. My pulse raced. The screech of tires on the tarmac was music to my ears.

Our arrival represented a demographic seismic event. How often does a human population swell 35 percent by the mere touchdown of a small plane? Before we landed, the Pihemanu census was fifty; now it was sixty-eight—not counting the Gulfstream crew—plus something like two million feathered friends. Twenty-nine thousand birds per person.

Several full-time residents helped load our gear onto golf carts for the drive to our barracks. The moment we were off the runway we morphed into an electric Moses, parting a huge sea of oblivious albatross as we inched our way along. Some birds acted like fans at a concert, dancing to the happy beat of their feet. Some mōlī strolled, some snuggled. Some threw their faces to the sky and squealed with delight, indignation, or triumph. Some rearranged their encampment. Some looked like blissed-out stoners. Brief skirmishes broke out over funny looks, unwelcome advances, and boundary violations. Half the animals were in motion; half were in a trance. Even as we walked the short path to Charlie Barracks, our boots passing within inches of their faces, the birds paid no attention to our grand population surge.

It was past midnight when we had a brief orientation and got our lodging assignments. The double bed in my second-floor room was a few feet from a bank of windows draped with black curtains serving an identical purpose as those of World War II London: avoid becoming a target. But here it was not about humans hunkering in basements. No. This was a wildlife refuge where the protected ones were *outside* and the enemy was *inside*. If we forgot for even a moment, Bonin petrels would start crashing into the glass. In fact, there were so many airborne birds it was surprising the ground was not already littered with casualties of constant collisions.

And the noise! Forget the Hollywood version of a lonely, faraway tropical island, forget Robinson Crusoe, forget befriending volleyballs. Midway is saturated with sound like the sea is saturated with salt. It's impossible to separate them, one from the other, or even to know which are mental interpretations. There was a constant choir of whistles, moos, clacks, whinnies, whistles, and shrieks. A continuous wind section accompanied the vocals. There were proclamations, atonements, and proposals. Was that someone knocking on my door? There were manic adolescent come-ons and tender reunions of mates. Did I hear woodpeckers, or were those cantering hooves? There were disputes over real estate and quick conciliations. Were those raindrops splatting on cement? I heard vigilant voices of protective parents and ecstatic exclamations of lovers. Were those sirens in the distance? I could have sworn I heard cheers from a football stadium and the contralto octaves of Phoebe Snow singing "Poetry Man." I heard holy men chanting at dawn on the Ganges. I heard an incoming chopper. I heard drums, lots of drums.

Breakfast at the Clipper House Galley was just before sunrise. As the sky got lighter, colors lost their nocturnal shyness and started strutting their stuff. White sand, shimmering turquoise water that turned royal blue outside the harbor, baby blue sky, and deep purple storm clouds in the distance. As much as the color, it was the motion. Lean, longwinged albatross sliced the sky into pieces of stained glass, window behind window, turning like a kaleidoscope in the firmament, hues and patterns in constant kinetic shimmering artistry. Everywhere, in every direction, on open fields and shining dunes, in ironwood groves and under native *naupaka*, were birds. Just beyond the galley, unmated mōlī trotted down a narrow path between shrubs, hurrying to the beach in a comic queue like Keystone Kops. Little yellow canaries flitted among them, a surprising introduced presence, the descendants of released caged birds. Black noddies wearing white skullcaps dutifully fed their impatient chicks.

Each member of the survey team was assigned a bike. Mine turned out to be an orange Panama Jack, a beach cruiser with balloon tires and a handlebar basket. It had brakes but no gears. A beer bottle opener was mounted on the frame, in case I died and woke up in Cabo. I slipped my faux-zebra-skin shower cap onto the seat to keep it dry. From that moment—though I didn't yet know it—I would be followed everywhere, in my most public and private moments, in every contained and open space, in every piece of clothing. It would involve an orifice—actually, every orifice—but it wasn't personal, if you can swallow that. (And, by the way, you will.)

We all had the same stalker; its name was *sand*. Sand that managed to be powdery and abrasive at the same time. Sand that seemed to thrive on friction. Sand that burrowed inside my socks and rubbed my skin raw, even after several washings. Sand that signed a long-term lease and took up residence in my ears. Sand that insisted on sharing my sheets. Sand that could make a saint swear like a drunken sailor.

Why was I surprised? I should've taken a clue from the English name for this island. With all these millions of glorious flying beings, you'd think, wouldn't you, that the biggest of three Midway Islands would be called—oh I don't know—say, Albatross Island or Mōlī Atoll? But no. It's called Sand Island. I rest my case.

We were issued paint guns, divided into three teams, and assigned a specific sector to start our counting. In the first few hours, my team of six women tallied close to ten thousand nests. We wove among albatross, trying to discern which birds were sitting on eggs and which birds were sitting on laurels. We squirted a dab of paint near each nest—not so close the bird accidentally ingested it, not so far the dab looked unrelated to the nest. The goal: neither overlook nor double-count. This got trickier when the wind picked up and the paint spray migrated. We skipped an entire sector because an endangered monk seal was napping among the birds; no one was allowed within one hundred and fifty feet. On the adjacent beach there were at least twenty *honu*—green sea turtles—lounging like lizards, all survivors of impossible odds. One female was so huge she looked like she could bench-press the pier, concrete pilings and all.

I wished I had her stamina. It turned out the hardest part about being on the Survey Team was not sand, physical exertion, or cranky temperaments. It was the burrows. Burrows that belonged to those Bonin petrels, numbering in the tens of thousands. The little feathered backhoes make it a practice to dig around and under albatross nests. You often couldn't see them until your foot suddenly collapsed a burrow and your legs went knee-deep in sand. I made rude noises every single solitary time because every single solitary time it was shocking, even when I totally knew it was going to happen. Since I never knew for sure if one of the eight-ounce excavators was at home, I followed the guidelines and started shoveling. Sand poured over the tops of my boots and through the threads of my socks. It snuck into my pants and up my shirt like a subway pervert.

It didn't take long for me to discover how much I hated falling. Every fall felt like a failure to me. I didn't care that the surface was soft. I didn't care that everyone was doing it. I didn't care that it was unavoidable. But whether I loved it or hated it, it's what I had. It's what we all had. All day I fell into burrows, most of which—praise Pihemanu—were vacant. But not always. One afternoon when I was on my hands and knees again, digging like a dog, I discovered two birds about ten inches under the surface. They were mates, doing their family planning. Can you imagine going along all la de da, like *honey let's make us a baby*, and then someone three hundred times your size steps on your spine? Naturally

Short-tailed albatross bachelor, Midway Atoll

you would lose the mood. For one thing, you can't breathe. Plus you're buried alive, your home is worth a lot less on the market, and a monster is snooping around in your love chamber. That's a lot of letting go.

After I interrupted their lovemaking, my job was to give the petrels access to air so they could scramble out from under the avalanche. When I succeeded in saving their lives, it turned out they did not appreciate my efforts. They thanked me by nipping my fingers and telling me off with verbiage I'd rather not repeat in polite company.

At dusk, hundreds of thousands of additional petrels dropped from the sky after their day at sea. For an hour the winged pinballs bounced from every imaginable trajectory and made joyful noises unto the heavens. They were darters, not unlike bats. After they landed, they sat patiently on the ground like they were expecting public transportation. When my headlamp glanced over them on my way home from dinner, several of the birds flew straight for my face. What am I, a bus?

It was Christmas morning. All eighteen members of the survey team dispersed for our first day off. As I pedaled into the wind on Panama Jack, inquisitive white "fairy" terns hovered over my head like angels scattering sacraments. Yellow canaries hopped from tree to tree, chirping cheerful ideas to each other. A highly endangered Laysan teal waddled across the path, her mallard-colored body distinct from her mottled head, as if she hadn't quite decided which outfit to wear for the holidays. Common mynas—superb mimics, all—stood in a circle clacking and whinnying, doing their best mōlī impersonations.

There was rumored to be a lone male short-tailed albatross somewhere in the avian masses. If so, he was a very rare bird indeed. Many years ago his species was clubbed to near-extinction in Japan, millions of magnificent creatures sacrificed for London ladies' hats.

When we wear feathers like crowns, are we hoping birds will abdicate to us?

I rode across the runway and dismounted when I thought I was in the vicinity of the short-tailed wonder. As I peered through my binoculars, a low-flying albatross slammed into the back of my head. I fell to my knees from the sheer force of the mōlī momentum. There was no pain, no blood, no blackout. There was this strange sloshing, though, as if my brain had liquefied on impact. I turned to look behind me, rubbing my scalp, half-expecting to see a knocked-out bird with cartoon stars circling his cranium. But I was in the middle of a mob, and there was no clue which bird had miscalculated my density. He must have jumped up after our wham-bam and hurried away without so much as a *thank you ma'am*. I must admit I was a little disappointed our intimate moment mattered to me and me alone.

Then, from my sandy seat in the grass, my thoughts returned to the short-tailed albatross. Looking around, I spotted him about two hundred feet away. He was huge. He had a waxen yellow head, a pretty pink bill, and a body of white feathers perfectly trimmed with black. There was nothing especially short about his tail. Despite the courtship frenzy going on all around him, he looked bored. The winds of the North Pacific did not cause him to hunker down, but the prospect of a girl did. His odds were long, very long. There may not have been an eligible female within a thousand miles or more. A few years ago there had been a brief flash in the pan for him, when two short-tailed girls were seen on Kure Atoll, about fifty miles away. Their eligibility status changed, however, when they decided to hook up with each other. The girls' relationship continues to this day.

Bachelorhood is a tiny obstacle compared to looming submersion. Current NASA estimates suggest a three-foot sea level rise by the end of this century. Gigantic weather had already happened. When the Japanese tsunami hit in 2011, all human inhabitants of Pihemanu retreated to the third floor of Charlie Barracks. The downy albatross babes had no such means of escape. When it was over, two hundred and fifty thousand chicks were gone. Half the entire population that year; half the class of 2011.

I wanted to honor them. Commemorating other species does not trivialize human loss—it adds paint to the palette. It colors outside the dark lines of grief and makes it more honest. It was nesting season, for example, when Midway was bombed on December 7, 1941—the same day as Pearl Harbor. Why not add the birds to our Memorial Day eulogies and commission mōlī sculptures among the marble monuments for lost men? I know we can't erase human tragedies, but can't we at least acknowledge the loss of other innocent beings caught in our crossfire? Are they not our brothers and sisters?

Pihemanu translates to "loud din of birds." In this case "din" doesn't merely refer to noise, nor does it translate well. Its origin may be the Sanskrit word *dhvan*: to roar, hint at, imply, make a noise, become covered, darken, allude to, envelop, or wrap up. A Hawaiian-speaking colleague recently compared the din of Pihemanu to the collective sounds at a boisterous wedding reception.

Among the Christmas expressions I heard were wolf whistles, insults, commitments, proposals, apologies, recapitulations, memorials, birth announcements, and dance invitations. I could have listened for years and still failed to comprehend all of what was being expressed. The majority of the sentiments came from Laysan albatross, but not exclusively. Handsome black-footed albatross stroked the lower chords amidst the high-pitched, swirling, chaotic music. They chanted a nasal *uh-oh, uh-oh, uh-oh* and trumpeted a note that sounded like "hey" in a sustained syllable that echoed from a faraway river canyon, shouted by a man who urgently needed to be rescued. To be honest, I couldn't be entirely certain whether some of the sounds didn't come from the reverberations inside my own banged-up head.

I didn't know if their calls were a warning, a plea, or a mantra.

I didn't know if I was saved or screwed.

I only knew I was being called.

Uh-oh. Uh-oh. Heyyyyy.

Uh-oh. Heyyyyyy.

Heyyyyyy.

Talia watches nesting albatross

I returned to Kaua'i from my stint at Pihemanu. In the end, the Survey Team had counted nests representing more than a million albatross, not including at least another million untallied non-nesters. A week after I got home I was invited to a small social function on a bluff where a few mōlī nested. At the event, the property manager introduced me to his daughter Talia. She read me like a book.

"Let me show you an albatross," she said. She was strong and slight and eight years old.

"Good idea," I said. As if I had never. As if I could ever get my fill. As if I had not just returned from their largest colony, from an island functioning like a magnificent centripetal force, condensing birds from vast open oceans onto a tiny atoll in the remote Hawaiian archipelago. As if I had not felt the wild comfort of their throbbing rock concert. As if I had not spent countless hours with them over the last decade on Kaua'i.

As if I had not searched for them all my life.

As if they had not guided me, lifted me, rescued me.

As if they were not my 'aumākua, my guardian ancestors, my guides.

Talia urged me to hurry.

"When's your birthday?" I asked as we headed toward a nest. I remembered very little about the language of third-graders.

"Earth Day," she answered. "That's why I love animals and why they're not afraid of me."

"That is so cool," I said.

"I can crazy climb trees," she said. "My mother says I'm part monkey."

"That is so cool," I said.

"If you trust me I can take a picture," she said, eyeballing my telephoto.

I slipped the camera strap over her head and showed her how to focus. Her first attempts were blurry. After that she fired away like a pro.

"What if I take a shot of you," I said.

"I gotta get Grace," she said, and ran to fetch her doll.

She settled under a mango tree and gently planted Grace like a seedling at her side. Talia knew how to stay far enough away from the bird, how to leave him undisturbed on his egg. She laid a comforting hand on her doll, which listed slightly toward the mountains.

"You make me feel happy," I said.

"I've been told I have that effect on people," she said.

The west side of Kaua'i was drawing unmated albatross from the waters of the Hawaiian Archipelago. When mōlī spotted the Pacific Missile Range Facility (PMRF), they dropped their webbed landing gear to take a look around. Eager to get their groove on, they searched for other singles. *Handsome bird seeks same. White with dark chocolate feathers. Must love children and like to dance. Squid breath a definite plus. Willing to relocate for a soul mate. Harassment calls from frigate birds will not be returned.*

Their nesting success became an issue at PMRF. Under other circumstances, the acres of the military base would have been ideal for the birds. There were northeasterly winds and there was easy access to the sea. There was a great runway for takeoffs and landings. Since the albatross census grew slowly, it took years to recognize the emerging problem: potential bird-aircraft collisions. All over the country, such collisions had become a more common occurrence. Scare tactics like hazing and pyrotechnics worked to scare off avian species at some mainland airfields, but they did not work at PMRF.

You cannot detonate the devotion out of an albatross.

Although it was legal for the armed services to "cull" the birds, a more creative deal was struck among several entities. As a military strategy, it was an uncharacteristically long-term approach. The US Navy, Fish and Wildlife Service, and Department of Agriculture came to an informal understanding with private landowners. Adult birds and eggs—and occasionally very young chicks—would be relocated from PMRF to approved properties on the north shore of Kaua'i.

Jason and Peter, federal wildlife technicians who worked at PMRF, began the daily practice of capturing adult mōlī. They placed the birds in dog kennels and loaded them onto the bed of their pickup truck. It took at least two hours to get to one of the release sites. Once the birds were set loose, they were free to fly back to PMRF—and risk getting captured again the next day—or choose other colonies to visit instead.

Just so, one bird found a place she liked better than PMRF. She was lucky; she scored the mate of her dreams there. In honor of her military association and the seventy-six on her leg band—which made me think of *The Music Man*—I named her Colonel Trombone. Naturally the pair would want to keep a consistent Broadway musical theme, so I named her mate The Librarian. Together they raised a healthy chick in 2010.

In 2011, when the pair reunited, they discovered an unexpected obstacle. In their absence, the landowner had built a predator fence that bisected their preferred nesting zone, an area of about one hundred square feet. Even though the birds knew how to land on both sides of the new fence, Colonel Trombone made it clear she preferred the west side, which was the safer side. The Librarian liked the east side better. He ultimately got his way that year, and they raised another healthy chick—just inches from the wire.

In 2012, their negotiations reached an impasse. Despite weeks of romantic nuzzling through the fence, they remained divided, like inmate and wife. If there was a conjugal visit, it did not result in an egg.

In 2013, I was relieved to see their nest had been constructed on the safe side. Colonel Trombone laid her egg. When it was The Librarian's turn to incubate, however, he simply could not commit. He sat on the egg, got off, crouched upon it, and jumped away, like it was a hot potato.

The Librarian faced a mountain of a marital moment. His concept of "home" was no longer the same as it was for his mate. Ultimately his internal map—which had led him with pinpoint accuracy to this tiny volcanic speck in the wide Pacific—was too much for him to override. He was 99 percent faithful to family, 100 percent faithful to his GPS.

In the sweet manner of his species, The Librarian stayed close to his egg. He talked to it through an opening in the fence, separated by mere inches, long after it went cold. He waited an entire month—about the same length of time his incubation shift would have been had he chosen to actually sit on his egg.

The Librarian and his dilemma

When Colonel Trombone returned from sea, her devotion was undiminished. She immediately went to their egg. The two birds chatted with each other, peering through the fence. A few days later, during a storm, the egg shattered under the mama. She spoke softly to the fragments and wandered a few feet away, dried yolk crusting her belly feathers.

Sometimes people chuckle when they hear this story, and make jokes about the birds' lack of intelligence. That attitude irks me. Who among us has not had an unsolvable relationship issue? Who among us has not been reluctant to let go? Seriously, is there anyone who has not incubated broken bits of a dream?

When Colonel Trombone and The Librarian returned in 2014, their luck ran dry. The Librarian was killed by dogs on the unsafe side. Since then, when Colonel Trombone has visited, she's plopped herself down in exactly the same spot as her previous nests. She has joined a few courtship boogies, but has not yet seemed ready to commit.

When she does pick a new mate, pray their GPS readings jibe.

Jason and Peter also had the job of gathering all the albatross eggs laid at PMRF. I joined them one day to take photographs for a magazine article I was writing about the program. We sat in their white pickup truck at the edge of a grassy field. To the west was the sparkling turquoise Pacific; to the east, the green Mānā plain. In the distance, brown ridges rose like uncurled fingers stretching toward the forests of Kokeʻe and the Waimea Canyon. It was a peaceful scene.

There were no noises from automobiles or machines, no airplanes overhead. The only sounds came from the easy flow of trade winds, the pulse of distant waves, the conversations of birds. Mynas chattered under a row of *kiawe* brush. Great frigate birds—ʻiwa—hovered in a cloudless blue sky. A lone western meadowlark sang from a corner fencepost.

Although the morning was already warm, Jason wore long sleeves and dark pants. He slipped on blue disposable gloves. His kind face belied the fact that his job was to be a professional abductor. He and Peter were the same men who caught and released Colonel Trombone and all the other adult birds. Today their job was to locate any new nests on the base.

We didn't need binoculars to spot the albatross in a clump of *aki-aki* grass. The bird's snow-white chest reflected the long angle of early morning sunlight; he looked like he was in a blissful state of meditation. I envied the bird's reverie.

I had tried to achieve his calm and detached state every morning for more than twenty years. My daily meditation sessions sometimes made a difference in how reactive I was to the stressors of the day, but I was always only one self-judgment away from the dismantling of my detachment. In an attempt to give myself some slack, I once took a month off work to go to a retreat site where a thousand people meditated and did hatha yoga together. Other than during sessions of chanting, the participants were silent for the entire month. We were silent at meals, on the walking paths, and in our dorm rooms at night. It was sweet to be freed from small talk. The absence of chatter allowed an intoxicating, expansive feeling.

But there was also a darker, more divisive force. Without the usual full-time work and twenty-four-hour on-call duties to corral my attention, the decibels of my mental criticism increased, which in turn popped the balloon of my bliss. I didn't like what I heard. Before the retreat I was unaware of how unrelenting and disparaging my thoughts could be. It was like listening to a recorded list of screw-ups—no matter how minor—from my entire life; when the list seemed complete, it looped back and started all over again. I found no easy means of escape.

The mōlī in the akiaki grass turned out to be Makai. He had hatched in that field twenty-five years earlier, grown up there, fledged from there. Years later he found his true love there. It was the only terrestrial home he knew. Makai and his mate, along with about eighty other pairs, had again returned to PMRF to nest.

Jason and Peter would find them all. They would take away their eggs. It was the best choice—and it was the only good choice.

I followed Jason as he strolled in the direction of Makai's nest. He gently touched a clipboard against the bird's belly. Makai jerked awake and snapped his bill. With one deft sleight of hand, Jason stole the solitary egg. With it went the only opportunity the papa would have for a family for another year. Sad, yes, but it sure beat the alternative. Makai did not know he could have been shot. He did not know his egg could have been smashed. He did not know his kidnapped daughter had just saved his life, and her own. He did not know she was about to be given to another family. It was a comfort to us to know that Makai was unlikely to stick around for long. In a few days he would return to the open Pacific for another year.

Jason and I joined Peter at the truck and drove across base to a humidified incubator. Peter knelt before it and placed his egg offering in a row of others, lined up like infants in nursery bassinets. Each embryo pulsed with paradox. Each was an orphan and a hero, a victim and a victor. Each was lost, each was found. Each was an ambassador to a new world, a native approach to an invasive problem. All without ever having hatched.

Before the eggs could be adopted, wildlife biologists Eric and Lindsay "candled" each egg with a flashlight. If they saw signs of life, they declared it fertile. When the eggs were all sorted, the scientists packed them into cartons and drove to the other side of the island. We arrived at a private colony two hours later.

The first adoptive parents were Rachel and Susan. Female-female pairs can be equally as good at chick-raising as male-female pairs, but unless one of them has spent an intimate moment with a male, there won't be a fertile egg in their nest. Like Makai, Rachel looked like she was in a trance. Her head was held high and her eyes were closed. You could easily imagine she was humming. You could imagine she was humming Jane Taylor's familiar lullaby.

Twinkle, twinkle, little star,
How I wonder what you are!
Up above the world so high,
Like a diamond in the sky.

Susan, Rachel's mate, was far out at sea, searching for food.

When the blazing sun is gone,
When he nothing shines upon,
Then you show your little light,
Twinkle, twinkle, all the night.

Lindsay reached under Rachel and removed her egg.

Then the traveller in the dark,
Thanks you for your tiny spark,
How could he see where to go,
If you did not twinkle so?

The biologist handed Rachel's egg to Eric. He saw no signs of life.

In the dark blue sky you keep,
Often through my curtains peep,
For you never shut your eye,
Till the sun is in the sky.

"No good," Eric said.

As your bright and tiny spark,
Lights the traveller in the dark,
Though I know not what you are,
Twinkle, twinkle, little star.

Lindsay chose an egg from the PMRF collection. She gave Makai's abducted daughter to Rachel. Rachel looked down at the ghost of her own baby. She looked down at the stranger occupying the spot where her baby had just disappeared. She spoke to her new child, with a voice soft and sweet. *Eeh eeh eeh?* She shimmied her body and settled back onto the nest.

Rachel closed her eyes. She offered herself completely to Makai's child.

In the same colony where Makai's egg got adopted, I watched two birds hang out in their own private corner of the woods. At age six or seven, Large Marge and Plenny Lenny may have been a bit too young to mate, but they were not too young to practice the art of courtship. They flubbed dance moves like teenagers rehearsing for cheerleader try-outs. They inhaled the sweetness of each other's scent. They preened and snoozed, neck-to-neck.

Large Marge jumped up from her nap and shook herself off. She trotted toward the bluff, Plenny Lenny on her heels. They chatted on the way, giddy with excitement. A storm! For birds who commonly cruise the Gulf of Alaska, tropical winds pose only the prospect of fun.

A dark mass of clouds body-slammed Kaua'i with torrential rain. Waterfalls appeared out of nowhere, gouging the vertical valleys of the

Nāpali coast. Flash flood warnings and small craft advisories were issued. Winds gusted at forty-five miles an hour. The Hanalei River overflowed its banks, gushing milk chocolate into the bay.

Marge and Lenny rode the bluster again and again, like a Six Flags roller coaster. It took no flapping for them to race downwind and glide back. They were young and fit; they could outlast almost anything the earth hurled their way. They squealed with delight.

In the meantime, the National Weather Service issued instructions for us humans to go home and stay put. Its high-water mantra was chanted on all the news outlets. *Turn around, don't drown.* By the end of the day, total rainfall would surpass any other twelfth of January in recorded history.

I watched the continuing deluge from the comfort of my house. Late in the afternoon I got the same message every household on the island received. Instead of a predictable warning, we got a legendary prophecy.

"This is your Kaua'i Civil Defense Agency." The standard opening was followed by a single sentence. "The sky is falling."

I am not making this up.

At first I didn't believe the message was real. I replayed it a few times until the electricity failed, wondering who among my friends could fake me out with a riff off the story of Chicken Little, and in such a perfect monotone.

Once I finally accepted the call as authentic, a whole new line of questioning opened up for me. Why would any civil defense agency (other than Oakey Oaks, Chicken Little's village) have a sky-is-falling option? Was there a prerecorded stable of messages for every catastrophic event in the world? If each message was original, was this one recorded by a rascally person whose parents read fairy tales aloud at night?

There was no further information. Nothing about when the sky was expected to land, or what we should do about it. After it fell, could the sky be recycled? Would it hurt?

I wondered if an earnest government employee recorded the call, eager to make light of heavy rain. The humor would not have been altogether inappropriate, since it was not truly a disaster—unless you counted hapless tourists who saved a pile of (Henny) pennies for a sunny Hawai'i vacation, only to find themselves in a monsoon worthy of Mumbai in mid-July. No homes or lives were lost, no injuries sustained.

When the electricity was restored, another robocall went out. "This is your Kaua'i Civil Defense Agency." I couldn't wait to hear what was next! A confession from Drakey Lakey? Would some poor worker get blamed for accidentally activating the message by pressing a secret code previously known only to Turkey Lurkey?

"The message you received earlier was a test message sent by mistake," the voice said, not without kindness. It then repeated all four guilty words.

"The sky is falling." The sentence hung in space like a decommissioned satellite. I eagerly awaited the next sentiment.

"Please disregard and we're sorry for any inconvenience."

Hang on! Disregard a falling sky? Forgive the inconvenience of a panicked Cockey Lockey running hell-bent toward the palace and scaring the poor king? Forget Foxy Loxy's appetite for the plump-breasted Gander Lander?

Then a final robotic request.

"Please do not call the police."

I thought I heard a subtle repentance in the tone, maybe even a tiny hint of humor.

If you read a book about albatross, it will tell you mōlī mate for life. And it's true, they do.

Except when they don't.

Ganesh and Gracie used to be an item; together they raised a healthy chick in 2009. After that, for unknown reasons—and for the next few seasons—they both had other mates: Ganesh with Lakshmi, Gracie with George. Like clockwork in the 2014 season, Ganesh returned after months at sea. Lakshmi reunited with him. In December she laid an egg. Both parents tended it faithfully.

Gracie also touched down, back from her own long-distance oceanic travels. Sadly, George never showed up. She could not know when or where his life ended. A presumed widow, she essentially had two options: resume her pelagic pursuits or hang around in the colony to explore the possibilities of a new partner.

Gracie chose neither. Despite acres of shaded woods and open fields, she constructed a nest next to Ganesh and Lakshmi.

In other words, Gracie moved in with her ex-husband and his second wife.

Could this be a ménage-a-tross? I shared my news with the biologist Beth Flint. Threesomes were not unheard of in mōlī, but Beth was eager to hear more and suggested I keep close track of the trio. Would all three birds participate in egg incubating and chick rearing? Why not? What child would not benefit from multiple sources of nurturing?

Gracie laid her own egg about eighteen inches from Lakshmi's. Was it fertile? If so, had she already found a new mate, or had Ganesh offered himself as a sperm donor? Only time would tell. After a few days, Gracie ditched her own nest and began taking turns with Ganesh and Lakshmi, brooding their offspring.

In the meantime, her egg sat stage left, mute and overlooked like an understudy memorizing her lines, never to hatch.

Alas, for some reason the three-parent egg also failed. Weeks past its due date, the big birds huddled a few feet away, not quite ready to give up. After Ganesh returned to sea, Gracie and Lakshmi lingered a while longer, preening each other, shoulders touching. Soon they both flew off for months of solo travel. Who knew what the next season would bring?

Once the 2015 nesting season began, it didn't take long to find out. Gracie chose to be close to Ganesh and Lakshmi again, but this time she gained a little more independence. She laid an egg about six feet away and stayed faithful to her own egg. Despite her commitment, however, we will never know if the egg was fertile. After five weeks without incubation relief from another adult, hunger stole Gracie's attention. She had to leave to sustain herself. If she had a new mate, he hadn't appeared for his turn. If Ganesh was the father, he already had Lakshmi's egg to incubate, and he couldn't be in two places at once.

The birds left more questions than answers. Would Gracie return to help feed Ganesh and Lakshmi's chick? Would she hook up with

Ganesh in the future? Did she have eyes for a brand-new pairing for herself, perhaps next time with that sweet, good-looking Lakshmi?

It made me wonder what *mate for life* really means to an albatross. Maybe it means passing on excellent genes. Maybe it means a rock-solid commitment for the survival of the kids. Maybe it means a rollicking reunion dance once a year. Maybe it means being punctual with meals. Maybe it means an occasional divorce, dalliance, or team-switch.

Maybe it means sexual preference is more of an active verb than a passive noun.

Why put mōlī—or ourselves, for that matter—into arbitrary camps that ultimately only serve to separate us from the truth? If we must classify others, why not create categories for qualities vital to our continued existence on this planet rather than waste energy worrying about who beds down with whom? Qualities like willingness to work hard, like authenticity and compassion, like unflinching devotion to the welfare of children and animals?

Our tendency toward categorization reminded me of a story about a family I know. Heather, Steve, and their three kids had moved into a home on the shores of a lake in Washington and were excited to discover a pair of bald eagles nesting high in the boughs of a red cedar next to the house. It was doubly fun when young eaglets were spotted in the aerie.

One summer afternoon, five-year-old Collin was sprawled on the living room floor, absorbed in the task of constructing a K'Nex Space Needle. When his mother walked into the room, she did not expect him to have bird sociology on his mind. Oh, but he did. Without looking up, Collin made an announcement.

"The eagles should have names," he said. "Parents first."

"What do you have in mind?" Heather asked.

"Trevor and Ethan," said Collin. He snapped another brick into place.

"If they're both boys, how did they get babies?" Heather asked.

Collin lifted his gaze, rolled his eyes, and rotated his palms skyward like a preacher summoning the Holy Ghost. His body language gave

Ola and Loa with one of their moms

him an air of authority, making him appear to be an expert on the biology of Trevor and Ethan's progeny.

"Surrogate," he said in three distinct syllables, as if enunciating for someone with insufficient intelligence. As if speaking slowly would afford his mother adequate time to comprehend an obvious concept. As if to say, *Who doesn't know this?*

"Of course," said Heather, admiring the mind of her five-year-old.

"Duh, mother," said Collin, going back to his Space Needle.

Because this is a tender albatross story I feel it's only fair to tell you, right from the start, the protagonists will die. Knowing the outcome may allow your heart to break gently, soothed by trade winds and gentle sunlight. It will also give you a leg up on me. I harbored hope for The Twins' survival, despite odds so impossible you could've tossed a stone in any direction and hit a wall called Never. When the little ones were wildly alive, the facts did not protect me. No, they did not. I fell in love, long shot or not, toes over torso.

Albatross girls always lay a solitary egg. No exceptions. Two eggs can be found in the same nest if the parents are a female-female pair, but they are usually infertile. If one of the ladies has briefly hooked up with a gentleman, fertility is possible. If both females have been with a boy, it's even possible for two eggs to hatch.

I asked Aaron, the navy biologist who oversaw egg adoptions, how often that happened. He could not find a single citation in scientific literature. Another seabird scientist said she had heard similar anecdotes twice. Twice out of millions of nesting birds over decades of data in dozens of colonies in more than twenty species. Even in the case of two eggs, it was presumed there would only be enough flesh on the belly of a parent to incubate a single offspring. A typical brood patch only covers twenty-five percent of one egg. The presumption is not often tested; female-female pairs usually pick just one; the other egg is rolled outside or buried within the nest.

Since albatross parents work nonstop to find enough food for one offspring, a pair of chicks would be inconceivably difficult to support. The Twins' moms were not willing to sacrifice either egg. It was risky, very risky. Could they find enough squid for any, much less all, of the family to survive? For more than eight weeks they took turns on the eggs, renewing their commitment with each changeover.

One rainy February morning I spotted shell fragments outside the nest. Had both babes actually hatched? I hunkered under my dripping umbrella and waited. Soon the mama mōlī stretched, exposing two downy adorable day-old chicks. They panted, exhausted from the labor of breaking free. The larger one raised his wobbly bottom above the rim of the nest and shot a stream of chalk-white guano. The mom angled her body, her tail pointing skyward and her bill touching the ground. She regurgitated a dribble of that high-octane squid oil. The babes sipped from her wide-open bill. She preened them. They peeped. She arched her back and puffed her chest, did a little shimmy, then settled down on them.

Who knew how they would behave as they grew? Most mōlī chicks on Kaua'i require a certain amount of personal space. When a boundary is crossed, the offended one squeaks and clacks until the offender backs off. No chick wants a pretender near his nest. No chick wants her parent confused about who's who. No chick wants to miss out on the smallest bolus of food. Would the bigger one shove his smaller sibling out of the nest? Hog their lunch? No. Anyone who knows albatross would bet large sums of money on amiable dispositions. Just as adult pairs nuzzled each other, so went the babes.

I dared to name them. This was foolish, if you think of pain as wrong. Names amplify sad songs. *Ola* and *Loa*. Hawaiian words that together meant *long life*.

To document feedings and try to identify at least one dad, I mounted a waterproof camera on an old cutting board and wedged it among ironwood roots. Gray and innocuous, the camera took a silent shot every ten minutes during daylight hours. Each day Ola and Loa were together at sunrise and sunset, so it seemed they spent the night together.

They preened, stayed close, looked around. Photos of them made my throat ache.

If you are like a lot of people, you might interrupt me now. You might ask if there wasn't a way to hand-feed the chicks. I would have to refer you to Aaron; feeding a seabird is more complex than feeding a songbird. You have to be trained and officially authorized to slurry a squid and force-feed a 'tross.

You might also ask whether The Twins should be euthanized to prevent their inevitable suffering. You might blame our species, and your own good self, for the many ways we've harmed the birds and their oceans. You might search for data to diminish your sorrow, to find a precedent. Alas, you will find little consolation in facts. None, actually. An albatross pair simply cannot catch and carry enough food to sustain two offspring.

We must try to be as brave as the babes, you and I.

Aaron put tiny leg bands on the chicks so we could tell them apart from others in the colony as they got more mobile. They might have henceforth been called twenty-three and twenty-four, but that never took. Ola and Loa didn't share a mother and likely didn't share a father, so they weren't even technically related. Even so, everyone called them The Twins, even scientists baptized in the stoup of statistical analysis. The chicks slept in the same bed and knew each other's heartbeats. They ate at the same time. They looked alike. Their movie was projected from a dual beam merging into a single image. Two moms, one courageous commitment. Two chicks, one impossible task. Two names, one meaning.

I didn't actually know their genders. I thought of Ola as male because his body was slightly larger. For the sake of balance, I called Loa female. Either way, I ran a 50 percent chance of being wrong. Their improbable presence melted any icy opinions I had about being inaccurate. What use are such cognitive constructs when two little furry babes bravely flap their wings in the face of death? To guess their genders was to honor their guts.

When she was about three weeks old, Loa grew into another kind of pioneer. She waddled away from Ola and tumbled down a six-foot embankment not far from her nest. At first I thought her trip was just that—she had tripped. I also found it difficult to believe she could climb back up the steep hillside. But I watched her take the fall and make the trek back up a dozen times over her short lifetime, webbed feet wide and wing-stumps spread for balance. Back on level ground, she went about the business of investigating leaves and shadows. She always returned to her more domestic brother.

Because it was an especially rainy winter, mosquitoes inflicted avian pox on most of the albatross chicks on the island. Nasty growths pimpled their bills and feet; eyelid lesions blindfolded them. Although others would later recover with residual scars, our little heroes spent the rest of their lives with obstructed vision. Their tubenose nostrils also appeared to be partly blocked by pox. There they were, two downy mōlī chicks, barely able to see or smell. Perhaps in pain, likely famished. As if they weren't underdogs enough.

Loa remained adventuresome and Ola soon followed. They never seemed desperate in any way. Since albatross chicks cannot forage for food, what did they seek on their outings? Loa tugged on low-hanging branches and caught raindrops. She sat on the bluff, facing a sea she could not see, still as a monk. She rocked back on her heels, webbed feet in the air, cooling herself and collecting her recommended daily allowance of vitamin D. One day I sat on the same ridge, not far away, facing the Pacific. A month-old bird and a full-grown human, nothing to say, nothing to do. I doubt she knew I was there. I tried to imagine her experience.

The wind, the mighty 'aumākua of albatross.

The warmth of the sun, the cool of the rain, the pound of the surf.

The eternal longing for a mother's return.

Loa reminded me of someone from long ago, back when I was working three jobs to put myself through graduate school. Inina was a four-year-old child with leukemia, isolated in a bone marrow transplant unit. Her name meant *glimmer of light*. Her family was from Guam; Chamorro was their language. The little bald-headed girl could not leave her hospital room for many weeks. I was her *a'amte*, her nurse. Just the two of us, eight hours a day, three days a week, with Inina in a hospital gown and me in my scrubs. I wore a mask. She taught me how to say, "Your breath stinks." *Haha poksen.* She stood across the room from me, her arms crossed, pretending to be mad until I called her "chrome dome." It made her laugh every time. When she liked me, I was *memmang,* auntie; when she didn't, I was *ataktak,* naughty. When she wanted me to feign offense, she tossed her favorite insult at me like a beach ball: *pantes pai.* I'm pretty sure she was talking about pie with filling of panties.

Where Inina found opportunities to play, adults saw mortality crouching in the corner. Sometimes she sat still like Loa, equal parts present and absent, looking out the window at her ocean view. Both the child and the chick seemed unafraid of dying. Death hovered nearby, inscrutable and detached. It never hid.

When Loa was six weeks old, she injured herself on her last tumble. I found her lying shivering in a light drizzle, one wing perpendicular to her torso. The ocean roared constant. I did what any nurse would do: I counted her respirations. They were shallow, gasping, and uneven. I yearned for some means of comfort for her. Across the valley, men hammered nails into the frame of a house. A rooster crowed. A shama thrush flashed its white rump. Dark clouds threatened. Ants marched steadfast. Loa kicked her feet in the air, trying to find purchase. A mōlī flew above us, grazing us both with a graceful shadow. "See that?" I said. "That's who you really are." I told her what a great job she'd done and how much I respected her courage. How hard her moms had tried. I sat down in the red dirt and wept. I wept for albatross drowned by long-line fishing hooks, for the ocean and squid and plastic; I wept for the winds, for the dreams they deliver and the dreams they blow away.

I wept for mothers who cannot save their children.

I wept for children who cannot save their mothers.

Loa picked up an ironwood needle with her bill. One last optimistic feat. One last assumption there would be another night, and in the dark a nest awaits, a nest that could use some rearranging. She had the most perfect toenails, black and shiny. On her broken wing were repeated dashes of white, like basting stitches. She was not yet fully sewed.

Before I removed his sister, Ola touched her with his bill, then got interested in a brown leaf instead. When Loa stopped breathing, I wrapped her in a towel and took her to a nearby wildlife refuge. When I opened the freezer, I couldn't help but think of a bizarre moment related to my sweet father. After he died of a heart attack nineteen years earlier, his body was taken to a funeral home. When we later realized his car keys had been accidentally left in his pants pocket, I drove to the mortuary to retrieve them. The funeral director handed me the keys. They were ice cold—and in that moment, my dad's death became real for the first time.

Alas, Ola was destined for the same outcome. I found his body three weeks later, lying in the shade about fifty feet from his natal nest. Adolescent birds danced nearby. They whinnied like horses, stood on tiptoes and pointed their bills in unison to the sky.

One chick had me worried. For weeks she was lethargic and smaller than the others. A medical diagnosis nagged on the periphery of my awareness, a nonspecific diagnosis we used for some infants and elderly: *Failure to thrive.* I remembered a few geriatric patients with their dry unfocused eyes, their listless limbs and disconnected spirits. The patients who seemed gone before their bodies were. The patients whose families procrastinated visiting; the patients who triggered profound feelings of helplessness in nurses. We had no effective medications, therapies, or interventions for them. When the patients died, it was usually a relief to know they were no longer so miserable. When they got better, no one could explain why.

Thankfully, one day the life force seemed to grab hold of the little chick. Maybe her papa had found the perfect squid and converted it to high-octane oil while he flew a thousand miles straight home. Maybe her mama sang her a song from her ancestors. Maybe she discovered her life's purpose. Who knew? After that, she kept getting stronger. She became alert and observant. She cocked her head like a spaniel when she watched butterflies and bees. She gained weight and grew feathers. Her wings got long. She stared out to sea, eager for every meal. She thrived.

I called her Onipaʻa: steadfast, firm, resolute. In the islands, it's loaded with history. Onipaʻa was the personal motto of the revered Queen Liliʻuokalani, the last ruler of the Hawaiian Kingdom. It also became the theme of The Queen's Hospital School of Nursing in 1917, when Her Majesty asked that the word *onipaʻa* be used by the school. It appeared on nursing pins in purple and gold, the colors of royalty.

I respected Onipaʻa for staying alive, for her verve. She had the introspective demeanor of a survivor of a near-death experience. She spoke little, except when one of her parents arrived. Albatross are often talkative. Parents speak to their eggs, chicks peep while they chip away from inside their shells, mates murmur sweet nothings, courting birds whinny to potential partners, adults shriek at perceived violations. When you hear an animated vocalization, it's usually intended for a recipient. The talker might be addressing a bird gliding overhead or standing in grass a football field away, but if you look around, there is almost always somebody. Seldom have I seen a 'tross talk to nobody.

When Onipaʻa was about four months old and still several weeks from fledging, she relocated to a new spot under a shady bush about fifteen feet away from her first nest. One day I overheard her having a quiet chat, like she was revealing the details of a fabulous secret. I couldn't see her from where I stood, so I quietly inched closer to spy on her. *Eeh-eeh-eeh.* She repeated herself again and again, clearly excited about something. No other bird was visible.

Then I saw the object of her affection: Onipaʻa was talking to an umbrella. Its fabric was decorated with kittens. There was a rusted stump where the handle used to be. The print was faded and stained from years of exposure to Kauaʻi red dirt. I could make out the brand, Giordano. The company's goal: "Make people feel great."

I had walked past that spot dozens of times over the years and had never seen that umbrella. Onipaʻa must have dug it up from beneath layers of forest debris. Once she found it, she not only invited the object of her curiosity *into* her nest, she *made* it her nest. Could any welcome

Onipaʻa and her umbrella

have been warmer? For the next several weeks she toddled to the edge of the bluff, flapped her wings and mimicked other chicks as she rehearsed first flight. Even when she got close to independence, she returned to her kitties. Guano evidence suggested she spent most of her time there. She remained true to their mutual home until one day she summoned all her courage and launched into the air, flying for the first time. I wished her every good fortune.

Nearly four years later, I was making my usual weekly rounds. When I looked over an old fence, I was surprised to see that kitty umbrella. I had not seen it since the summer of Onipaʻa's fledge. In her absence, it had gotten reburied in vegetation. Now there it was, exposed again. Next to the umbrella, chatting away, was Onipaʻa. She had returned, after years at sea. She had not forgotten her feline friends.

A few years ago, as the nesting season was coming to a close, more than one hundred chicks were near the end of transformation from fuzzy footballs to peerless pilots. Some jumped into the sky, trusting something good would come of it. Some waited for brisk trades and were lifted like prophecies. Each traveled as both noun and verb. "Fly" on the wind was not just what they would "do" the rest of their long lives; it would also be their address, their ancestor, their altar. They would stay aloft on the two universal wings of life: self-effort and grace.

Sadly, several chicks did not survive. One Friday in late June two unleashed dogs burst into a colony, barking and breaking necks. Eight babes died on the scene. Five more were injured, and in a sense they became orphans. Not because their parents were dead, but because they were dead to their parents. They would be gone, taken for care, and their parents would be unable to find them.

It was a gut-wrenching scene. Because we got there shortly after the dogs, and because a rehab team was able to accept the birds, a few of the injured chicks were alive the next week. Cooperation among private landowners and government agencies covered the costs. Seabird biologists exchanged recipes for feeding the chicks. Households and hotels delivered hundreds of towels necessary for the chicks' care.

Despite their wounds, despite their reputation for poor survival in captivity, despite physical and psychic shock, despite traumatic separation from everything they knew, despite the fact that they would likely not see their parents again for many years, four of the chicks lived. Only one of the five died, his brain damaged from a head bite. The others gained weight. Several weeks later they were released onto a federal refuge. All four fledged.

The colony attack may have been senseless, but it did not turn out to be useless. If dog-bit albatross chicks in cages can create a selfless human collective, imagine what a selfless human collective can create.

No, seriously. Imagine.

Two

Promising

MY MOTHER WAS DIAGNOSED when I was in third grade. I wasn't used to her being out of commission, not for any reason. She led my Bluebird troop, was active in the PTA, gave piano lessons, and sang in the church choir. Surgery barely slowed her down, but it did leave a long dark scar and a hollow vacancy on her chest. Because she was a nurse, she thought it best I knew the facts about radical mastectomies. She made her own ordeal seem effortless. She sometimes called her prosthesis "thesis" and used feigned declaratives like, "You can lead a horse to water but you can't write his thesis." Sometimes she whipped it out and lobbed it in my direction. She gave the impression breast cancer was a lightweight challenge—like the macaroni art we crafted in Bluebirds—and not a panic button.

My parents had recently purchased our first television. They let my sister and me watch only three programs: *Howdy Doody*, *Captain Kangaroo*, and *Mickey Mouse Club*. I was over the top about the Mouseketeers, but mostly I was riveted to Annette Funicello. It was her smile, of course, and her kind eyes. She made everyone seem welcomed to the club. Even now when I look at her photo, I feel her mysterious power. But her real wizardry to me was just south of the big ANNETTE on her T-shirt. Among Mouseketeers, she alone was growing bosoms. If she could do that, I thought, so could my mother. She could summon another breast. The void could be filled—it could happen. Birds grow new feathers, don't they?

I wanted desperately to keep her magic coming. I don't know how my seven-year-old brain equated that magic to money, but I decided to send her some cash. Back then my allowance was five cents a week. In order to save, I had to fight off the temptations of Tootsie Rolls, baseball cards, and comic books. When I finally had ten nickels, my mom and I rode our bikes to the bank. I asked for the best fifty-cent piece they had.

The search wasn't as simple as I imagined. I didn't like the most common coin, the one with Benjamin Franklin. To me, Ben looked like a cranky cow. No, I wanted the Lady Liberty half-dollar, the one with the bald eagle on the back and the sunburst on the front. I liked how Lady L. beckoned with her hand, the way a friend might. Plus she had exactly the right number of breasts.

I don't recall what I said to Annette in my letter, but I remember my dad helping me tape that coin to the stationary. I might have gotten discouraged had I known she was getting six thousand fan letters a week in those days.

Sometime after that, I got a note from her secretary. Let's say her name was Betty. When it came in the mail, I took it to my pigeon loft to read, comforted by the cooing of black-barred racing homers. Like my mom, I loved birds. When a neighbor boy outgrew his flock and offered them to me, along with the little structure that housed them, I was thrilled.

I was wearing red corduroy pants and a plaid flannel shirt when I read the letter. I didn't care if I sat in bird poop. Inside the envelope was my Lady Liberty fifty-cent piece. Betty quoted Annette, telling me I needed the money more than she did. She said Annette was very happy I was a fan and thanked me for the generous gift.

I adored that letter. Not because the coin represented more than two months' income for me, but because it made it seem like I had magic on my side. Now, all these years later, I adore it for its unadulterated compassion. Annette was kind for no good reason. She was kind, even though neither of us knew my mother's life would end soon. Annette personified the love they talked about in church, something I never felt there. Maybe it was possible to feel unconditional love on hard pews in a scratchy dress, but it hadn't happened that way for me.

I wasn't alone in my feelings about Annette. Many people, men and women both, now tell me they had a crush on her. They usually blush and apologize, like a crush is nothing, a meaningless puppy love. But how can it be nothing when it gives a child a rush of hope?

I will always honor the human that was Annette Funicello. To me she was a shining light, a sanctuary and a navigator. She was my talisman.

It was just past dawn when I awakened to the quiet sound of my mother's voice. "Honey, I need your help," I heard her say from the next room. She was forty-one, I was nine. She was a volunteer nurse for the participants of a summer church camp. I didn't know why she was calling me, and it was cold in the old unheated lodge in northern California where we shared two tiny rooms. Her bed was inside. Mine was outside, on a screened-in porch. I loved the sounds of the occupants in the hills above Russian River. Ravens, Steller's jays, and barn owls flew in and out of those woods; raccoons and deer roamed the forest floor. They were all members of my inner circle.

I wrestled with my clothes in the sleeping bag so I could get dressed without letting in too much chilly air. When I got to my mom's bedside—not more than fifteen feet away from mine—she pulled back the sheet to show me her leg. From the knee up it looked like a regular extremity; from the knee down it looked like an eggplant, shiny and purple. I'd never seen anything like it. My mom told me she had fallen on the path coming home the night before. She had been playing piano for a few counselors, singing spirituals like "Do Lord" and "He's Got the Whole World in His Hands." Just before my bedtime I got to ham the lead to "Dem Bones Going Rise Again" because I'd memorized all the verses.

> *The Lord He thought He'd make a man*
> *Dem bones going rise again*
> *He took a little water, he took a little sand*

The walk back to our quarters was downhill, but it wasn't steep. To this day I don't know how my mom made it back to our room without assistance.

> *He took a rib from Adam's side*
> *Dem bones going rise again*
> *To make Miss Eve to be his bride*

I don't remember her mentioning pain, or who I found to help us. My dad was at work, a hundred miles away.

> *Put them in a garden fair*
> *Dem bones going rise again*
> *Thought they'd be most happy there*

I do remember her being carried by a man to a station wagon and us driving down the winding dirt road to a doctor's office in Guerneville.

> *Around the tree the serpent slunk*
> *Dem bones going rise again*
> *And at Miss Eve his eye did wunk.*

After that, things never returned to normal. Never.

> *Apples, peaches, pears and such*
> *Dem bones going rise again*
> *But of this fruit you must not touch*

More times than I can count, I've agitated over what would have happened if I'd awakened when she got back to our rooms that night, if there was something I could have done.

> *Lord came down for a look around*
> *Dem bones going rise again*
> *Spied dem cores all over the ground*

My mother was a pragmatic woman. It was 1958. She would have known there was no urgent medical care within driving range. She would have known there was no good reason to arouse people when nothing could be done until the morning.

Adam Adam where art thou?
Dem bones going rise again
Here I is Lord, I'm coming now

Still, it's hard to imagine her being able to sleep. What was going through her mind?

Adam you must leave dis place
Dem bones going rise again
And earn your food by the sweat of your face

Did she have a spooky inkling about a bone metastasis from her breast? How could a sober young woman break her leg so easily otherwise?

Put an angel at the door
Dem bones going rise again
Said y'all don't come 'round here no more

Shortly after that, I began to address my mother by her first name.

Eve took the needle, Adam took the plough
Dem bones going rise again
And that's why we's all working now

I started calling my mother Beatrice.

A few weeks later I learned the truth about Beatrice's condition from a creepy, blue-eyed doll named Toodles. A neighbor girl took the red-headed thing everywhere she went, so I called them Big Toodles and Little Toodles. Big Toodles thought she was some kind of ventriloquist. She said anything she felt like saying, then blamed it on her doll. It was twice as stupid because her lips moved when she "threw" her voice. I didn't hang out with them; in fact, I pretty much dodged all girly things. Nothing was more boring to me than the idea of playing dress-up and faking tea parties. Dolls were the worst. Their curly lashes, spooky hair follicles, and rotating arms scared the heck out of me.

The street was where the real fun was. Flag football, kickball, and baseball were the top sports in my neighborhood. My playmates used expressions like *hey batter hey* and *ground rule double*. *No chips* meant the hitter who broke the window was supposed to pay for the window.

Plus there were other fun things to do. I rode my green Schwinn Tornado to the local graveyard and caught blue-belly lizards, salamanders, and garter snakes. I snuck downstairs to the bowling alley in the small local shopping center and scrounged for lost coins so I could play pinball.

Big Toodles and I did have one thing in common: our mothers were friends. They concocted ways to get us to play together. Beatrice said it was good for my character. I didn't care about my character. Big Toodles loved calling me Tom. She thought she was Einstein for coining an abbreviation for tomboy. It irritated me, but I pretended it didn't. I forced myself to conjure an image of Tom Terrific on *Captain Kangaroo*. Who wouldn't love to be a kid with a magic cap that could transform you into anything? With that cap on my head I figured I could turn Big Toodles into cat poop.

My grandmother, a retired Presbyterian missionary, fretted over my nickname. "Whistling girls and crowing hens never turn out right in the end," Granny Ruth warned. She had recently come to stay with us and had no shortage of opinions about my behavior. She said I should wear my hair in a perm. She said I should take my hands out of my pockets. She said I should eat all my dinner and if I didn't, she would show me her photos of starving children in China. I never understood how emaciated kids with no pants were supposed to make cauliflower edible.

I told Beatrice I hated Big Toodles. Beatrice was devoted to pediatric wellness. She quoted from Dr. Benjamin Spock's *Baby and Child Care* like it was the New Testament. Matthew, Mark, Luke, Spock.

"No, honey," she replied, "You don't hate her, you hate what she did." Talk about confusing. How do you hate the mouth that mocks you but stay friends with the owner of the mouth?

Big Toodles spilled the beans on my tenth birthday, but of course she pretended it was Little Toodles who did it. Beatrice was in the hospital. My dad Chuck was taking me out for my three favorite birthday presents: a hot dog, a root beer float, and a horseback ride. A woman from our church had a rickety ranch we were allowed to visit. A ride on a horse, even on an old bony animal like Dogwood, was my idea of a good time.

I was excited. After I put on my Annie Oakley vest, holster, and hat, Chuck and I hopped into our Rambler station wagon and went straight to the A&W drive-in. Oh, the sweet delicious pleasure of that frosty drink bubbling down my throat! The hot dog was grilled and sliced in half lengthwise, just like I guessed real cowgirls would prefer. Somewhere on the road after lunch, Chuck turned the car back toward home. I don't remember if I asked him why. When we pulled into the driveway at our house, the curtains were drawn. I opened the front door to a dark room. A bunch of girls in party dresses, including the dreaded Big Toodles, shouted, "Surprise!" Oh, I was surprised. Freaked out, more like. When I got Chuck alone in the kitchen, I asked when we were going to the ranch. He smiled and mussed up my hair. "We're having a party," he said. Anyone could see he was proud to pull off such a great secret.

Fortunately for me, not all the attendees were doll-girls. Chuck had invited Joanne Felizianetti. I liked her. For one reason, she straight-armed boys when she ran for touchdowns in flag football. She was in my Bluebirds troop until we mutually "flew up" to be Camp Fire Girls. Camp Fire was one of the only places where being a girl was totally fun, where we hiked and paddled canoes and pitched tents. We had week-end campouts. When I was old enough, I planned to go for a Wohelo Award—the equivalent of Eagle Scout—in Aeronautics. I liked building model airplanes.

My birthday party did not have model airplanes. It had frilly dresses and lots of screaming. To this day I do not understand why girls scream so much.

When he was serving cake, I told Chuck I wanted to call Beatrice. We talked every day. He told me they moved her to a room without a phone. "Why?" I asked. I wasn't sure he heard me over all the squealing. Big Toodles shoved Little Toodles in my face to make it look like the obnoxious thing was speaking. She spoke in her trademark high-pitched nasal voice.

"Because your mother is going to die, Tom," said Big Toodles. She smirked, evidently amused by her doll's keen observation skills.

My parents raised me to say something nice or say nothing at all.

So I said nothing.

Then I socked Toodles in her smirk.

She screamed.

My ancestors first arrived in Hawai'i in 1832. Richard and Clarissa Armstrong sailed from Massachusetts with the Fifth Company of missionaries. The newlyweds were both twenty-six years old, and the trip was supposed to be their honeymoon. When they left the harbor, they didn't know Clarissa was already pregnant.

Many years later she wrote about the arduous journey. "We came on a whaling ship with wretched accommodations. I was seasick most of the whole voyage of six months, sometimes partially suffocated for lack of fresh air in the stateroom below deck, which I was unable to leave. The water sent forth such a bad odor that one must hold the breath or cover the nostrils while drinking. The whole scene rises up before me as a sort of Purgatory. Surely no man but in ignorance could ask a woman to go with him in such horrid surroundings as the whale ship *Averick*, with an intemperate commander. And no woman but in ignorance could consent to go without violating the command 'Thou shalt not kill.' I look back and wonder that I lived."

After being stationed on Maui for several years, the Armstrongs were transferred to Honolulu. Richard served as the pastor of Kawaihao Church in Honolulu, where he officiated the wedding—in English and

Hawaiian—of Queen Emma and King Kamehameha IV. Both Richard and Clarissa were dedicated to education, and Clarissa offended church leaders by inviting Hawaiian men to classes that were supposed to be for women only. Coming from a family of professionals, she was accustomed to making her own decisions. Her brother was the chief justice of the Massachusetts Supreme Court; Clarissa was a teacher. It was not long before she and Richard withdrew from the mission so Dr. Armstrong could accept the post of Minister of Public Instruction under Kamehameha III. Clarissa later published *Reminisces of a Missionary Chair* (Murdock & Company, 1886) written from the perspective of a rocking chair that accompanied decades of their work.

Clarissa's life was destined to guide me back to Hawai'i six generations later. Her firstborn, the child who was in utero for those awful six months on the *Averick*, later became known as Caroline Beckwith. She was the grandmother of my own grandmother, known to us as Granny Ruth. Granny Ruth's cousin Martha Warren Beckwith was an eminent scholar who conducted extensive research in Hawai'i. In addition to *Hawaiian Mythology* (Yale University Press, 1940), she completed *The Kumulipo: A Hawaiian Creation Chant* (University of Chicago Press, 1951). Both books are still in print.

I was three years old when *The Kumulipo* was published; the author was eighty. Although Granny Ruth spoke often of her cousin, I was probably in Auntie Martha's company four or five times in my life. She died when I was ten. As far as I know, only one photo of her remains. When a librarian at Vassar kindly sent me a copy several years ago, I was startled to recognize my clear resemblance to her; in fact, her face seemed to be a composite of all the women from my mother's side of the family. She never married or had children. Her memorial tribute cites her "single-minded devotion and courage."

Since I had only vague memories of Auntie Martha, my esteemed ancestor's appearance in my dream in 1979 will forever remain a mystery to me, and the greatest of gifts. It was she who would lead me back home, she who would show me where I had gotten lost more than twenty years earlier.

Home by the light of the moon

A few weeks after my nightmare birthday party with Toodles, I sat in class fidgeting, waiting for the school day to end. I needed a distraction. Mr. Pagni, my fifth grade teacher, was an enthusiastic educator. Sometimes when he lectured, a dot of white spittle formed on his lower lip and bobbed there like a seabird on an ocean swell. When he pressed his lips together and opened them again, the dot stretched like a rubber band, then snapped to his upper lip. I made hash marks in my notebook, recording spit migrations. How many more minutes until the bell? I was in a big hurry.

My uncle was in town, which was a rare treat. My mother's older brother was known to the neuroscience world as Dr. Theodore Holmes Bullock. I thought he knew everything about every species of animal ever studied, like the *nudibranch*, which I loved to say, and others I was embarrassed to mispronounce, like *sea anemone* and *orangutan*. I daydreamed about becoming his research assistant and heir apparent, camping on the shores of Lake Tanganyika and muttering comments like "Dr. Livingstone I presume?" Although it was only October, I had already asked my parents for a pith helmet for Christmas. Because Uncle Ted was a comparative neurophysiologist—whatever that meant—I wanted to be one too. Decades later he wrote a book called *How Do Brains Work?* As an adult I tried and failed to make sense of sentences like "Subthreshold oscillatory potentials have been hypothesized to generate temporal neuronal coding."

He was a great storyteller and folded his signature absurdity like origami into every tale. When he said something was "perfectly satisfactory," he meant it was fantastic. A person with sloppy clothes practiced "studied insouciance." The glassed-in aviary of tropical songbirds in his home was the "Bullock bestiary." I couldn't imagine better indoor entertainment than the constant movement of curious beings flying from perch to branch in the living room.

Uncle Ted had the hairiest eyebrows I ever saw on a human being. In the noonday sun they cast shadows upon his eyes, not unlike window awnings. I'm serious. If he was self-conscious about them, I never heard him say so. Because I wanted him to think me witty, I teased him about those brows, pretending to fret over the disappearance of a beloved pair of fictitious pet caterpillars. Like an improv comic, he picked up my grounders. He feigned offense. "You mean Lophocampa and Maculata?" he answered, using the Latin name for the moth of a hairy caterpillar. We didn't laugh. We thought it was funnier to pretend it wasn't funny when to us it was actually very funny.

The previous night Uncle Ted and my dad Chuck had discussed current events at the dining room table. They supported desegregation, so naturally I did too. The Yankees had just beaten the Braves in the World Series, so I knew we would dissect RBI averages when I got home from school. Everyone in my family was a fan of the San Francisco Giants, but who could dislike Yogi Berra?

Finally the bell rang. When I remember hurrying home from school that afternoon, I see homes one at a time, in slow motion. The houses in our 1950s suburban tract were small, identical, and close. I don't remember if anyone swept a porch, if a car drove by, if a dog barked. Everything except me was motionless. I burst through my front door like a half-grown retriever, all legs and fetch. For reasons I didn't understand, there was a family assembly in the den. Granny Ruth, Uncle Ted, and Uncle Burly were there. Chuck was home from work earlier than usual, and my sister Marcia was already home from school.

Uncle Ted looked around, searching the walls for new data. Lophocampa and Maculata twitched. Chuck stared at his feet and rubbed his hands together. When words finally emerged from his lips, I could barely hear him.

"Your dear mother," he mumbled, "passed away today."

I waited for more. There was always more. I wasn't entirely confident I knew what passed away meant, but I instantly knew it was a bad thing. Granny Ruth looked like she might collapse under the weight of a heavy yoke. Uncle Burly blinked fast, in uneven staccato, sending signals of grief with eyelid Morse code. Marcia was speechless. They were good people, all of them, and kind. But for some reason, no one touched anyone.

It took me decades to stop looking for the hugs that went missing that day.

Marcia went to her room and closed the door. I went outside to look for a playmate. I found my neighbor Nicky digging an underground fort in his backyard. We crawled into a six-foot hole under a tarp and pretended we were snipers firing at soldiers from the USSR. We drew a penis on the plywood wall, then—out of fear of being busted—drew a pile of cannonballs so we could say it was a cannon. By the time I got home, maybe two hours later, my family was already behaving as if everything was normal. The memorial service was scheduled. There was no wailing, no gnashing of teeth. No one hit anything, no one blamed anyone. No one said "cancer," much less "dead." It wasn't done, not in my family, not in 1958.

As was expected of me, I went to school the next morning. Mr. Pagni gave an assignment to the class, then pulled his chair up close to mine.

I told him he smelled like graham crackers. When he asked how I was doing, I already had the correct answer memorized. "Fine," I said. He pressed his lips together and searched for comforting words. He congratulated me for being so brave. He said I had to be strong. When he told me God must have wanted my mother, I decided God was not to be trusted.

Being strong evidently worked for Chuck and my uncles; it didn't work for me or for my sister. It didn't work for Granny Ruth either. In the remaining years of her life, she never really recovered from the loss of her only daughter. She never stopped asking God to explain, the God she spent her life serving.

There is no such thing as a good time for your mother to die. I've heard it helps if you're mature enough, and have been given time to prepare. But I've been around a lot of dying people in my career, people of every diagnosis imaginable—people who were sick for decades and people who were struck down an hour before—and never once have I heard a child of any age say, "This would be a good time." There's always another time, a theoretical better time. People speak of their moms, saying she should have died earlier, with her husband. She should die later, after she apologizes for being so terrible. She should die, but only after she's forgiven her own mother, or has one more surgery, or one more round of chemo. Just not right now.

If you're very young like I was, there's another dimension. I adored my mother. I adored her too much to be a separate being. Virtually everything I did was a reflection of her. If she was dead, how could I not be dead too? I lost my footing and my weight; I became a cloud of ash swirling over a foreign landscape, my compass spinning, my clock broken.

An animal's ability to process time is evidently inversely proportional to its metabolism. Smaller critters process light faster than larger ones. Images move faster, time moves slower. A fly dodges your swatter because the fly's brain gets information four times faster than your brain. You swing the swatter with all the force you have. The fly sees. Freeze. Framed. Action. In other words, time does not fly for a fly. The older we humans get, the slower we see details and the faster time seems to move.

For an eighty-five-year-old, life speeds by. One moment ago she was in school. One second ago, he was a soldier. The opposite is true for a child whose brain works on full tilt. Everything gets boring fast.

Beatrice's death happened for me in reverse time-lapse. The concept that I would never see my mother again was way past my navigational reach, beyond gravity and tides. It would've been easier for me to flap my arms and fly to Mars. I had no landmarks, no stars, no wind. Instead of condensing months into moments, like watching a papaya seed grow into a fruiting tree in a few seconds, time expanded in the other direction. In my mind Beatrice died slowly, moving in reverse, from tree to sapling to seed, one realization at a time, one denial at a time. Death was named wrong like a sunset was named wrong. Everyone knows the sun does not really set, but it seems safer than acknowledging that the earth is twirling and hurtling through space.

In order to stay alive, I had to find a way to be a separate organism from my mother. I had no choice but to give her demise some kind of false scaffolding. If she was gone, there could only be one conclusion: I had been bad. Very bad. I had been so bad no one would ever say what it was I did, not out loud. I would have to figure it out myself, even if it took my whole life.

I made a promise to Beatrice, a promise that instantly became my personal puppeteer. I vowed I would reverse whatever I had done. I vowed I would bring her back to life.

One morning about a year after Beatrice died, I was getting ready for school. Chuck appeared at the bathroom door while I was brushing my teeth. He reached into the medicine cabinet, rubbed a dab of Brylcreem in his scalp, and ran a comb through his hair. He wore a brown suit with a bright red tie.

"Ask you something?" he said. I leaned over the sink and tried to spit with authority, like the Dodgers' pitcher Sandy Koufax. "Shoot," I said, wiping my mouth with the back of my wrist. In sixth grade, I thought that sounded cool. It was 1959. I was eleven years old.

"You remember Virginia," he said. He seemed a little tentative. Was he blushing? I did remember Virginia, sort of. Chuck had had dinner with her, maybe once or twice, but I didn't know what for.

"Do you mind if I get serious with her?" he asked. I didn't understand why he was bothering to ask me. I thought he meant he wanted to have a serious talk. Serious, as in Sunday morning sermon. Serious, as in a President Dwight D. Eisenhower speech. Why would I care?

Next thing I knew there were wedding bells. There's nothing like your father making goo-goo eyes at the altar with a strange woman while you're in full-on denial about your mother being permanently gone. To make matters worse, he spoke a vow with Virginia in the same sanctuary he spoke a eulogy at Beatrice's memorial service. Of the two events, the wedding was harder. By far.

There were six of us in the formal photo in the sanctuary: Chuck, Virginia, her kids Danny and Madeline, Marcia and me. Chuck wore the only real grin on the dais. He looked like he thought he was the luckiest man in the universe. The rest of us, including the bride, looked like we were barely holding it together. I was miserable. Virginia was already trying to turn my head in feminine directions. I had a bad perm, which to me was a redundancy. I wore a dress with one of those horrible scratchy petticoats. I posed with my feet perpendicular to each other, the way girls were supposed to, at least according to Virginia. I felt ridiculous. How could you field a grounder standing like that?

We moved out of the only house I had ever known. The house where real mothers live. I was suspicious about where all this was going, but I kept my mouth shut. I wanted so much to be like Chuck, to be fine, to go with the flow, to be funny, to never show anger or fear. In reality I was shaken like a carbonated bottle, utterly confined, ready to burst. Relief had to come from somewhere. It happened a few months after that horrible wedding, on April Fool's Day. My prank was filling the sugar bowl with salt. It was the kind of thing we did in the house where real mothers live.

When Virginia put the "sugar" on her grapefruit and took a bite, she made an awful face. She yelled at me, got up from the table, and slapped me across the face. It was the first time in my life I had ever been hit. I was stunned and infuriated. My body was barely able to handle the rage, but I took it to school and somehow held it there. That night after dinner I begged Chuck to come see me in my room. The lights were out when he got there, so I must have already been in bed.

"How could you marry her?" Out from the pressurized bottle shot a baffled little bird, trapped too long, lost in space, no direction known, furiously flapping, seeking shelter in the dark. I sobbed, I begged him to explain, to make sense of it, to tell me he'd changed his mind. I wanted us to wake up from this nightmare. I wanted us to ditch Virginia now, tonight, this minute. I wanted us to go back to our real house. I wanted my real mother back. Beatrice was bound to turn up. What if she couldn't find us? In my eleven-year-old wisdom, I informed Chuck that Virginia was too different from Beatrice for things to work out between them. I told him Virginia wasn't kind, that she wasn't fun. I told him she yelled at me. I told him she spat when she yelled. I told him she wasn't smart, that she referred to gnats as "gah-nats." When I told him she had hit me, I thought the deal would be clinched. I thought he would pull down the suitcases from the garage storage and start packing, once he knew.

Chuck listened. He listened to my fury, my grief and desperation. He watched me, his little flailing bird, as I spiraled from the sky and crashed into the whitewater of my pain. He tried to explain, my gentle father did. He rolled with me. He did not tell me to snap out of it. He did not suggest I was overreacting. He did not mention it the next day, or ever again. He simply had confidence I would get over it. He had faith. He loved Virginia. He thought she was fantastic. They stayed married for thirty-five years, until his death.

It never dawned on me to hate Chuck. I thought I hated Virginia, but mostly I hated her occupancy of Beatrice's rightful throne. It took a long time for my resentment to cool. When it did, it cooled very slowly, one-tenth of a degree at a time, and was always subject to flares. It helped a little that I could make Virginia laugh. It helped that I liked Madeline and Danny. It helped when I started calling her Virg. Lots of other people started to call her Virg too. There was a hint of affection in the nickname, but it didn't mean I'd reneged on my promise to Beatrice.

No it did not. It meant I was tolerating a pretender. It meant I was bid-ing my time until Beatrice came home. Virg couldn't help it if she had a fatal flaw. She couldn't help it if she wasn't Beatrice. Because she wasn't Beatrice, I could not accept her. I could not accept Virginia without betraying my mother. I could not accept Virginia without breaking my promise to bring Beatrice back. My promise to make her undead. My promise to undo whatever I did that killed her.

Years later when it dawned on me that some of my friends had abu-sive parents, I began to see Virg in a better light. I began to recognize how destroyed she was when she lost her brother to war, her first hus-band to a secretary, her mother to cancer. I realized what an impossible job she inherited when she married Chuck. She suddenly had four kids under her roof—all between the ages of eleven and fifteen—and two of those kids saw her as a dangerous usurper.

Virg was a nonjudgmental soul. When she caught me smoking Marlboros behind the house when I was in seventh grade, she simply told me to quit. When I got busted for shoplifting in high school, she and Chuck picked me up at the police station and drove me home in complete silence. When I dropped out of Cal Berkeley for a year so I could work my way through Europe, she asked for postcards. When I spent one thousand dollars—left to me by Granny Ruth in her will— on a red Triumph motorcycle, Virg bought me a matching red helmet. When I graduated from Cal and moved off the grid to build a cabin without electricity in the Oregon woods, she and Chuck hammered a few nails. When I decided I would be more employable if I started nurs-ing school instead of going to grad school in ornithology, she thought it was a good idea. When I married Paul in a spontaneous hippie wed-ding, she sent blessings. When I divorced Paul to be with Sherry, Virg took it in stride. When I pulled up roots and moved to the home of my ancestors in Hawai'i, she sent her *aloha*.

Paki didn't know it, but she was about to get a substitute parent too. When it was time for her to hatch, her shell began to feel like a

Paki, one week old

straitjacket. She was eager to unfold her wings, to smell the ocean, to stretch her legs. She wanted to see the sky. She wanted to see her mother and father. She could hear them talking through the wall that separated them. She replied with a few tiny peeps of her own. She tapped the inside of her shell with the tip of her bill, again and again, until she punctured a hole. She was greeted by the sweetest Hawaiian breeze, so tiny it tickled. A pinprick of sun spotlighted her face. Falling asleep, she waited for enough energy to take another punch at her shell. When Paki succeeded in creating a hole the size of a quarter, her mother took a peek through the hole and spoke softly to her.

In that moment Paki learned about love.

She watched her father as he carefully peeled off a fragment, a tiny chip of her day's work, holding it in his mighty flesh-tearing bill like a jeweler would hold a diamond in his tweezers.

In that moment Paki learned about tenderness.

It took three days for Paki to finish her breakout. She fell to her side panting, exhausted and wet. For a while the lower half of her shell clung to her bottom like a calcium bedpan. When she was finally able to extract herself, when she was able to wobble upright, her mama bent down and regurgitated a small stream of squid oil. Paki put her head into her mother's open bill and sipped from the stream.

In that moment Paki learned about service.

She got many small sips of oil from her parents in the first several days of her life. She grew stronger and more alert. Most of the time she napped beneath one of their soft warm bellies. One morning when she was nine days old, she felt her mother stand up. Paki had no reason to be alarmed until human hands scooped her up. In her distress, she vomited and kicked. The hands wrapped her in towel, put her in a box and carried her away to a waiting vehicle. She would never see her biological parents again.

In that moment Paki learned about heartbreak.

She had no way of knowing what the hands or voices meant. She had no way of knowing what a human was, much less a biologist. Nothing smelled familiar. She had no way of gauging how long she was in the towel in the box in the truck. She had no way of knowing that the hands were saving her from an even worse fate.

After some time the hands picked up her box and carried her to a nest. They lifted her off the towel. She kicked. In front of her an albatross stood up and exposed her egg, a dead egg, an egg that was not destined to hatch. The hands gently removed the egg from the nest and replaced it with Paki.

Paki's new mother looked down at the absence of her egg. It was forever gone. In its place was a downy disoriented baby. She looked at Paki and spoke. *Eeh eeh eeh?* She settled on her new child, right as rain. She accepted Paki wholeheartedly. If she had sorrow she kept it to herself.

In that moment Paki learned about surrender.

I was in my last semester of undergraduate nursing school when all my classmates and I were scheduled for routine faculty evaluations. The sessions were in fifteen-minute blocks. On the posting, I noticed mine was the only thirty-minute appointment. I was secretly tickled, thinking they were going to commend my superior scholastic and clinical aptitude.

When I walked into the office, Trudy and Margaret—the nursing instructors—were already seated. They were solemn women, so I didn't really anticipate friendly banter. Neither could I have predicted what came next. Margaret slid a pile of "critical incident cards" across the table toward me. Each 3 x 5 card had a handwritten comment beneath a preprinted question: *What did the student do that was effective/ineffective? (Circle one)*

My stomach sank. In all, there were thirty-five cards in that stack.

"Please read them," said Margaret.

Every one of them had "ineffective" circled. Three of the cards were titled "Appearance." One card faulted me for standing too close to a sink when I washed my hands. One said my white shoes looked scuffed. One reprimanded the way I wore my nursing cap. (Few nurses wore caps anymore, but ours was still required. We students mocked it, pointing to its uncanny resemblance to a dog bowl.)

The heading on the remaining thirty-two cards was "Inappropriate use of humor." The instructors described event after event they had personally overheard, all relating to me laughing with patients or hospital staff. None of the incidents had been mentioned to me prior to that appointment. The actual content of the humor was moot. None of the incidents cited me for crude, cruel, or demoralizing language. It was simply not the way a professional nurse behaved, they said. To be effective, nurses needed to keep a cool distance. Humor was too familiar, too intimate, and would not be condoned.

I was devastated. The midterm evaluation was a fist that socked my worst vulnerabilities in the gut with a perfect combination of crippling punches: it cited my wrongdoings, held me powerless to undo them, and came as a surprise.

It also came with a veiled threat.

"We're not trying to get you kicked out," Margaret said at the end of our half hour, looking over her bifocals and smiling with thin lips.

Sure feels like it to me, I thought to myself. I found out later her statement was a dishonest reassurance, one that exposed the very intention her words denied.

In that office on that day, I was ten years old again, guilty of matricide, about to lose everything. When I showed up for school the next several days, my eyes were red. I stayed silent in class unless I was asked by Trudy or Margaret to speak. After a few weeks, when an uncharacteristically animated Trudy approached me in the hallway to tell me she thought I was doing much better, I understood what she and Margaret wanted. If they couldn't get rid of me, at least they could keep me quiet.

That was not, thankfully, the end of the story.

In the twenty years after graduation from nursing school, I worked in several settings, finished a master's degree, founded a pain management program at The Queen's Medical Center in Honolulu, published several articles, and was regularly giving national talks about humor and health.

One evening after a long day at work, I was relaxing at home with a glass of wine. When the phone rang, my partner Joanne answered it.

"For you," she said, shrugging as she handed me the receiver. The caller's voice was unfamiliar to her.

"Hob?" asked a woman. "This is Trudy." I had not seen or heard from either of my nemesis instructors, not once in two decades.

"We're having a big anniversary celebration at the school," she said. "We wanted one of our grads to keynote, and we thought of you." She wondered if I would be available to fly there for the evening festivities. The school was twenty-six hundred miles away.

I asked what topic she had in mind. I wanted to hear her say it.

"Humor, of course," Trudy said, as if she felt the answer was obvious. Did I hear her (almost) chuckle? "Humor in health care." I repeated her request aloud so Joanne would know what I had just heard. It was unnecessary; she had already figured it out. Both of us had anticipated this ironic moment.

From Trudy's tone, it sounded as if she had no recollection of the appointment that shattered my spirit and eventually crystalized my concept of the vital role humor played in hospitals.

I did give that keynote several months later. I wouldn't have missed it for the world. Remarkably, both Trudy and Margaret were in the audience. So were several of my classmates, most of whom were aware of what had happened to me all those years ago. In my hour-long presentation, I wove in the story of that fateful midterm conference. I used it as an example of positive growth in nursing, of how far we'd come in our willingness to be truly human with our patients. Although the gala gave me a golden opportunity to stick it to my ex-instructors, I did not publically denounce them. The way I saw it, there was much more power in withholding negativity.

My revenge was subtler. My revenge was in letting them know I had not forgotten, that they had failed to silence me, and that I was still laughing with patients.

When I was immersed in clinical data in graduate school, I decided it would help me to gather facts about Beatrice's illness and death. If only I had more information, I thought, maybe I would be released from my shame. Maybe I wouldn't be so averse to making mistakes, any of which felt potentially lethal. Maybe details would set me free.

I wanted to know everything, the sequence of events, what medications my mom got, if she was in pain, and how she handled fear. I wanted to know if she had accepted her terminal state. I wanted to read progress notes written by her nurses during her last weeks of life. I wanted to know the source of her courage. I imagined I could collect those specifics the same way I assessed my patients. The more clues I got, the closer I'd be to a good treatment plan.

I had a very limited pool of reliable informants. Granny Ruth was long gone. My uncles tried to help, but they couldn't remember much from the events nearly three decades before. Beatrice's medical records proved impossible to obtain. Marcia, who is two years older than I, had some bits of information. Chuck turned out to be my key resource—he had good recall and was kindly willing to dig through his memories.

For the better part of a year I sent him questions. He answered them, returning long letters in his even-tempered, impeccable handwriting. He knew dates and streets and doctors' names. He knew clinical terminology. He thought he knew how Beatrice felt and he knew how he felt. Several times during the course of our correspondence he mentioned the depth of the faith he and my mom shared. Never was it put to a greater test than in Beatrice's last days.

"The night before your mom's death she was obviously quite ill, and expressed the question about whether she was terminal," Chuck wrote. "She told me her only regret about dying was leaving her family. Just a short time before this, she also expressed disappointment that the San Francisco Giants were not doing too well in the National League. I tell you this just to point out that she never lost touch with the world, as well as experiencing compassion for others. Bea's classmate from nursing school at Berkeley came to stay with her, and I did not go to work the next day to stay in close touch with her condition. She telephoned me in the morning to say that Bea had lapsed into a coma. I went to the hospital immediately. When I arrived, she had already expired. The event was not a surprise to me, although one always has hope. I wasn't angry or afraid. I seem to have been born with trust in God's presence, love, and goodness, as well as belief in immortality."

When I read that last sentence, I knew his words were the truth for him. Chuck's words sometimes sounded like platitudes, but with him they were real life. I've never known anyone like him, anyone as consistently aligned, mouth to heart, words to deeds. It was how he lived. There was peace in that realization, but the real revelation for me came in a later letter.

"I should also thank you and Marcia (how did I fail to do this before?) for reflecting firmness and strength to me during that time," he wrote. "You showed that strength mainly in the calm way you accepted the news of her death, your response of kindness to Granny Ruth, and your continuing school without interruption. You and Marcia went on with daily life as normally as possible, and this was of considerable help to me. My feeling was, and is, that you exhibited commendable strength of character beyond your chronological age. Much of this was the gift of your mom's care for you, shown all during the years she was with you."

Wait, what? Chuck had been fooled by my "strength of character" act? He was pleased by the calm way I accepted the news? He was convinced, not unlike my fifth grade teacher, that I was fine? The first time I read his words, I was critical of his inability to see how destroyed I was. I wondered if he knew me at all. But as I watched my gentle papa age, I got progressively glad I had pretended to be fine. All those years I'd felt like a failure at helping my mother, until I learned to be satisfied with knowing I'd actually helped my father instead. That became—and remains—good enough for me.

A tall young woman hugged a blue cooler to her chest as she walked across a ragged pasture in misty rain. With her long limbs and sorrel hair, she looked like she belonged among grazing geldings. I halfway expected her to swish flies with her ponytail.

Horses couldn't have been further from Fawne's mind. She had only one focus, and it was inside the cargo in her arms. She spotted me on the bluff and waved. When she arrived at the nesting area, she put down the container and lifted the top. Since this was my first time watching a translocation, I was surprised at what I saw. My career had been spent in a modern medical center, so I imagined a living albatross egg to arrive in a bleeping high-tech portable incubator with settings for temperature, oxygen, and humidity. Shouldn't it be swaddled like a precious newborn inside a cushioned carriage worthy of its grand lineage? Nope. Try bubble wrap in a plastic Costco cashew container.

Fawne unwrapped the contents and squatted in front of a male whose nest was already known to hold an infertile egg. She gave him a gentle nudge with the cooler lid. He rose obediently. Nimble as a blackjack dealer, Fawne whisked away his egg and replaced it with a good one. She backed away. He watched her, looked at his new child, then sat back down. Fawne and I lingered a while, admiring his astounding acceptance.

It turned out there was something else on Fawne's mind that day, a story I didn't know until years later. "I looked healthy, but inwardly I was in agony," she said. "I was really tired and couldn't think." She was only twenty years old at the time. Fawne had been in college in California when she found an insect bite—with a red circle around it—on her body. She was diagnosed with a staph infection and given antibiotics, but they didn't help. She started losing her memory. "It freaked me out," she said. "I didn't have the faintest idea what was being said in my classes."

Even before a Lyme spirochete was identified as the culprit, symptoms forced Fawne to drop out of school and retreat to her parents' home on Kaua'i. It hid in her system for a long time. Fawne got varying opinions about what was going on. "They told me you have cancer, you're depressed, you're hormonal." Her discomfort only got worse. "Once I was in so much pain I had to go to the ER. They said I was fine and I should go home. I knew it wasn't fine."

Even though she wasn't much of a TV watcher, her disease forced her to consider new options. "I was watching *Mystery Diagnosis* and this guy had an experience exactly like mine." She had no idea Lyme disease had been a consideration. She read everything she could find until it all came together: the bite, flu symptoms, hot joints, headaches, and exhaustion. After a four-month wait, she got an appointment with a physician from the Lyme Literate Doctors list. "It was the first time someone sat down and got to the bottom of it. That started my long journey on high doses of three kinds of antibiotics," she said.

The disease and its treatment took Fawne to darker places than she'd ever known. "I had no hope," she said. "There was so much pain and I was so beat down. I was constantly devastated." There was no relief in sight. Then her neighbor Joseph—the same friend who had invited me to visit the albatross on his property—suggested Fawne start shooting some videos. He knew she loved photography, so he loaned her a camera.

"At first I was just glad to be in nature," Fawne said. Despite her difficulty concentrating, she managed to read portions of Carl Safina's book *Eye of the Albatross*. "I got blown away at their will to survive," she said. "When a squall came through, it all passed. I said to myself okay, so I'm in the middle of this storm. Like this was just a little fragment of my life and I can get better again."

When I asked Fawne about the source of her strength, she gave credit to her parents and her boyfriend. She also said the birds helped her live vicariously. "When I saw the mates reunite, I could feel the love those two birds felt for each other. I fell in love too." Over time her connection grew even stronger. "When I was with the birds it was a place of peace. I got some time off from all the suffering." She started going every day. When the fatigue was overwhelming, she took a nap in the colony. "They became like my closest friends. They just accepted me as I was," she said.

It took a while to recognize the birds as healing for her. "With them I could get out of my own story," she said. Prior to that she felt like her diagnosis had become her identity. "I had to go on disability and it was the most humiliating experience of my life," she said. It was hard for others to comprehend the impact of her disease. She had to convince professionals she was still unwell. "I'm like, are you kidding me? Do you think I *want* to live on the couch? I had to go to court hearings with binders full of literature and test results to prove to them I was sick." She needed their authorization to continue treatment. "You're feeling like you're going to die and they tell you to get a job," she said. "They tell you get over yourself."

Finally, after many months, her symptoms started to plateau and her blood counts improved. Her renewed energy allowed her to consider the impact of the albatross on her recovery. "Around the birds there weren't any words, but I felt totally understood," she said. "You know what's funny? They weren't trying to help me. I was me and they were them. They weren't reflecting my Lyme disease story. They weren't reflecting any story." They were, she said, simply allowing whatever was happening.

"That was what I needed. I didn't know it, but it's what I needed." She thought back to that day we met up on the bluff. She remembered how easily the incubating bird accepted the adoption.

"You know what?" Fawne said. "I think I was just like that egg."

The birds had accepted her without constraint. They had no interest in her story or her illness. They simply allowed Fawne to be there, to shoot a little video footage and take a few naps. That was more than enough for Fawne.

Recently the National Weather Service reported a bizarre cloud formation moving erratically over southern Illinois. The "biological targets," as the NWS called them, turned out to be a huge swarm of monarch butterflies migrating south. Despite risks related to drought and dwindling milkweed, they were headed to Mexico. If you're an insect that weighs less than a postage stamp, how do you even consider a trip across the border? What if your brain is no bigger than the tip of a pencil, then what?

Laysan albatross are gargantuan compared to monarchs. Still, you'd be hard pressed to get a radar image of them unless they've gathered to feed at some mass squid spawn or the smorgasbord surrounding a factory fishing ship. At sea there is nothing albatrossian that resembles flocks of finches, parliaments of owls, or murders of crows. "Colony" is a collective term, but it refers only to the time they spend on the ground during nesting season. In other words, about 5 percent of their lives.

To make an accurate map of meandering albatross, you have to be a scientist with permits and access to a sizable colony. You have to capture and release a few parents, then wait for the birds to return with data. The good folks from Oikonos Ecosystem Knowledge, Pacific Rim Conservation, and the US Geological Survey (USGS) accomplished all these tasks in the summer of 2014. They taped temporary lightweight GPS tags to the back feathers of a dozen birds and tracked them over a time span of seventy-nine days. They assigned an individual color to each bird and superimposed their flights on a map. The visual result: bright multicolored lines—each line depicting the travels of a single bird—extending over a vast expanse of ocean.

I showed the map to a few friends, and it turned out to be an interesting Rorschach. One person saw strands of candy, sweet and full of promise. Another person saw a frightening pattern of ocean depletion and pelagic plastic. One person saw the earth exhaling, another saw a fire. One artist saw an image of colorful streamers billowing in the wind. He was most impressed with how the birds' origins and destinations were always the same. "What's most mind-blowing," he said, "is not the fact that they can fly such long distances but that they find their way home at all." Like dozens of swifts diving down a chimney to roost, the streamers converged, swirled, and disappeared into a single point, signified on the map by a bright yellow star.

Of course, the birds' real destination was minuscule, and much smaller than the yellow star made it appear. The actual geographic location on Kaua'i was a fenced bluff at the edge of a botanical garden with an area smaller than an American football field. About forty pairs of birds nested there, and dozens of subadults came and went, searching for the perfect mate. With such easy access to the trade winds, it was a great spot for a colony. There was no need for a runway. The birds simply walked to the cliff, spread their wings, and were summoned heavenward. Once airborne, they banked north toward Alaska.

If the distance from Kaua'i to the southern Aleutians is roughly two thousand miles, and the birds' east-west foraging range is about the same, the colorful streamers were billowing over an area of about four million square miles. Compare and contrast: the entire United States is 3.8 million square miles. In other words, to find food for their chick, *a pair of Laysan albatross may search an area the size of the entire United States.* Talk about your hardworking parents.

Even though traveling such distances is unimaginable, the feat is trumped by the extraordinary fact that albatross can find their way home in such an empire. If a pyramid can be declared a Wonder of the World and a person can be anointed a saint, shouldn't there be awards for nature's most astounding achievements? The competition would be crazy, but if I ever got a chance to serve on that nominating committee, I would lobby for albatross navigation. Ask yourself if you could find a few tiny acres in so many millions, especially if you had no landmarks to guide you. Of course you couldn't; none of us could. Even if you were a sea captain with a sextant and a feel for celestial guidance, Pacific skies are often layered with clouds, so steering by the stars would prove difficult anyway.

We humans are just starting to learn how it is we can find our way across town. The 2014 Nobel Prize for Medicine was awarded to three scientists who discovered the mechanism of our inner GPS. They described "place" and "grid" nerve cells that are responsible for giving us an idea how to get places without having to consult Garmin at every turn. Their first clue to the discovery came from studying a rat's brain. If we can learn about wayfinding from caged rodents whose ancestors have lived in captivity for hundreds of generations, imagine what we could learn from the wild, long-distance travelers among us. Author and conservationist Carl Safina spoke of their many talents. He described how dolphins and bats virtually image a high-definition sonic world, in darkness and at great speed. "Many creatures," he said, "blow us away with sight, hearing, smell, response time, diving and flying capacities, sonar abilities, migratory and homing abilities." The list goes on.

What if albatross don't find their way home with their brains? Even if they steer by the earth's magnetic field, magnetoception doesn't tell the whole story. Even if they're guided by what they smell, their olfactory expertise doesn't complete the picture either. Plus there's the matter of timing to consider. Not just time of year, but the rendezvous time coordinated with mates whom they presumably have not seen for months. How do they know whose turn it is on the egg, and whose turn it is to feed the baby? Even if we think "instinct" alone entirely answers the question, that doesn't mean instinct itself isn't a miracle.

Maybe the birds match each other's frequency. Maybe they visualize the outcome they want and follow that vision. Maybe they just go with the flow, trusting wind, gravity, stars, smells, and magnetism to guide them. Maybe they are swayed by stories they hear from other birds. Maybe they find their way home with all their hearts, guided by love. Who can rule out any of these possibilities?

Just like they are rooted to their place of hatch, I am anchored to certain immutable truths: when and where I was born, who my ancestors were, what my primary culture admires and abhors, what wars exploded, who broke my heart. All these details sleep in my bed with me, beyond my awareness and more central to my life than I can possibly imagine.

Old friends of mine, a married couple, volunteered for a medical mission many years ago. They adopted two infants from Bangladesh and brought them back to the United States. One daughter did well, but the other was troubled. By the time Maria was fourteen, she was regularly skipping school, using drugs, and doing her best to get pregnant. To prevent her from running away, my friends had to sleep on the floor outside her bedroom. When she did manage to escape, Maria often mysteriously wound up at the city train station. Her exhausted parents ran out of viable therapeutic options, so they took her for a visit to Dhaka. They hoped her birth home would ground her and give her a sense of belonging. They sought counsel from the adoption agency. When the representative opened their file, my friends discovered an astonishing fact: their daughter's biological mother died in childbirth. She had been living in a train station.

Maybe my primary job is not much different than Maria's, or that of an albatross. Maybe I don't have millions of square miles to navigate, but I do have countless judgments that keep me from finding my way home. Home: a place I belong, a place where I am forgiven and forgiving. A place where I am authentic, where I laugh, where ancestors visit my dreams. A place where there is justice. A place where swifts can dive down chimneys and butterflies have all the milkweed they need. A place where birds lead the way.

In order to do my job, I had to be vigilant for predators—some human, some mental. People have judged, manipulated, scared, and angered me.

They have inspired guilt, caused me to lose sleep, blamed me, underestimated me, lied to me, wasted my time, hurt and betrayed me. But my own mind has been more than an equal coconspirator: it has judged, manipulated, scared, and angered me. It has inspired guilt, caused me to lose sleep, blamed me, underestimated me, lied to me, wasted my time, hurt and betrayed me. If I want to stay above all that chaos, I have to lock my wings like a switchblade and fly steady—albatross style. Most days the task seems impossible.

But isn't impossibility a crucial aspect of any pilgrimage? If it were easy, I wouldn't value it. It has to be unfathomable. How possible is it for a monarch to migrate across a continent? For an albatross to find her chick on a tiny volcanic rock in the most remote island chain in the world? When I consider the challenges my fellow beings face, how can I not emulate their creativity and courage?

As author Dani Shapiro says in her book *Still Writing*, "We cannot afford to walk sightless among miracles."

I strolled on a grassy Kaua'i bluff not far from the colony of the GPS tracking project. Hanalei winter waves thundered below, fogging the air with salty mist. Above the bay, sculpted mountains reclined like green goddesses carved by eons of tropical storms. Waterfalls plunged down their glossy necklines.

An albatross glided through the haze, solitary and stunning. He disappeared around the bend just as quickly as he appeared, as if his visa allowed him only a few seconds on this side of the veil from an alternate universe. I looked around me. A devotee like me is always eager to recruit new disciples to Albatrossian practice. Alas, there was no one within preaching range. Then, as if on cue, a potential prospect entered stage right.

"What was that?" a woman shouted. Her authoritative voice made her question seem more like an official complaint than a friendly query. I turned to see her leaning out the window of a rental car. She pointed

Laysan albatross glide on seventy-inch wingspans

in the general direction of the bird's flight path. I approached the vehicle and extended my hand. The woman's flaccid handshake contradicted her commanding tone but did not dampen my enthusiasm. No. When it comes to mōlī, I am part dancer, part jester; part Isadora Duncan in "Blue Danube Waltz," part Baloo the Bear in "Bare Necessities." I flung a few wise petals at her feet and began telling her of albatross long lives, high fidelity, and masterful navigation. I had hardly gotten started before she interrupted me.

"But what *good* are they?" she said, getting out of her car. I stepped back, intimidated by the sheer height of her. She must have been over six feet tall. Did I hear a German accent? Her tone was a hybrid of accusation and condescension, as if she was addressing someone who needed scolding for using expressions like *irregardless* and *mute point*. Her ballistic bosoms pointed in different directions, which I found disorienting.

Frau Krankyhosen, that's what I imagined her name to be—Mrs. Crankypants.

Other than her handshake and the disparate directions of her breasts, nothing about Frau Krankyhosen was ambiguous. Her Maggie Thatcher hairdo made me feel like I should salute something. A pale mustache sat motionless above her upper lip like a rider on a Lipizzan stallion. She quoted lines from *Rime of the Ancient Mariner*. She invoked Samuel Taylor Coleridge and spoke of the poet with palpable devotion, like he was still alive and could not keep his two-hundred-year-old hands off her twin peaks.

Our discussion about the epic poem was twenty-first-century civil, with each of us throwing down the gloves of educational credentials and spiritual convictions. The Frau called upon orthodoxy; I referred to ornithology. She spoke of mathematics; I mentioned mystery. She name-dropped Berlin. I shot back Berkeley.

I even tried humor, which was foolish. I knew the rule: people laugh with people they like. If they don't like you, you aren't funny. Still, I believed in the transformative power of the birds. I told Frau Krankyhosen about an albatross that once tried to incubate a volleyball, and another that chose a decoy for a mate, remaining faithful to "her" for a couple of years.

When I saw no hint of a smile, I should have bailed. But no. I went even further out on the proverbial limb. I told her about how I had included those same funny stories one night at a local library when I was giving a talk. I told Frau Krankyhosen about an audience participant who interrupted me to challenge my overestimation of albatross intelligence.

"How can you claim they're so smart if they try to mate with fiberglass?" the man at the library asked.

I was ready with my reply. "I don't know about you," I said, "but I consider myself smart." I paused, making meaningful eye contact with people in the crowd. "When I was younger I made a few bad choices in the mate department. Things might have worked out a lot better if at least one of us had been unable to speak."

The library audience had a good laugh, I told Frau Krankyhosen.

She stared at me, annoyed by my little tale.

"In other words," she said, "that bird has no purpose." She folded her arms under her bosoms for emphasis. The right side of her mustache twitched, migrating in the direction of her nose, trying to escape through the closest orifice. By that point I'd gotten a little fight-or-flighty myself.

In the end, the storied bird was just that to Frau K. It was a story, and not even a good one. Since the albatross had no place in the food chain of her understanding, she knew where I should hang it. Over my head, dead, a confessed burden around the innocent white neck of humanity.

I was tempted to end the conversation with a quip worthy of the dowager countess of Grantham, but I couldn't think of anything. So I surrendered—not because it was over, but because it was useless. I had failed to convert a nonbeliever. No matter what else I said, I wouldn't have been able to change her mind.

That, I decided, was a job for the birds.

Not far away, a family of mōlī faced an unusual issue. At first glance their mellow nursery didn't look like a crime scene. Monterey Jack was self-absorbed in the manner of happy children everywhere. He entertained himself, fumbling with bits of ironwood like a toddler fumbles with blocks, for the feel of it, for the fun of it. It reminded me of playing pick-up sticks with Beatrice, sitting on the living room floor.

At ten weeks old, Monterey Jack was hefty for his age. His dad Jose Manuel napped in the shade with his bill tucked under a folded wing. His mom Juana Cota was at sea. Both parents were novices at child rearing, but they were doing a fine job finding food for their fast-growing boy.

As I watched them, a flash of light caught my eye, a glimmer on the ground. There, next to Jack, was a flying fish. It looked fresh. It was intact—except for its missing head. The upper spine poked out from the carcass like a skeletal metacarpal pointing a finger at the guilty party. I had seen a flying fish on the ground once before, years ago. As with Jack's fish, it was one head short of whole. The discovery of a critter outside of its usual element was a bit disorienting, like seeing an endangered Hawaiian monk seal dozing belly-up in the middle of sunbathers on a crowded beach.

I had a working hypothesis about that first fish. Perhaps it had been dropped by a red-footed booby harassed by a frigate bird. Such intimidation happens commonly on Kauaʻi, and is why frigates are categorized as *kleptoparasites*. Their Hawaiian name ʻiwa means thief. So when the fish fell from the sky, I figured it just so happened to have landed in the albatross colony. Right? Mystery solved.

Or so I thought. Watching the scene, I kept looking for subtle hints. For one thing, the assumptions did not line up as well as they should. Jack's nest was upwind from prevailing trades, which would have blown a tumbling fish *mauka*—toward the mountains—rather than onto his nest. Plus he was under tree cover. It did not seem physically possible for the fish to have plopped down at our boy's feet. If it wasn't a red-footed booby that dropped it, how did it get there?

Jack did not feast on the flesh lying next to his bed. Perhaps it didn't occur to him it was actually food. He was accustomed to regurgitated squid, pureed to oily perfection. What good is a raw bony fish with pectoral fins as wide as wings? Jack ignored it. His dad ignored it too.

Despite his seemingly innocent slumber, Jose Manuel became the primary suspect.

When Juana Cota returned, all hell broke loose. She tore into her mate, squealing and biting. Jose Manuel beat a hasty retreat, waited a few minutes, and then returned to her side. He leaned in, preened her neck, spoke gently to her. He seemed to want forgiveness, or at least a truce. She was not ready to grant either one.

The plot thickened. Innocent as he was, Monterey Jack was not spared his mama's wrath. She grabbed him by the neck and shook him. He cowered like a dominated dog, dropped eye contact, and whimpered. I had seldom seen a parent act like this. I'd seen them be fiercely protective, to be sure. But who was she protecting, and from what? Was she upset by the fish and simply venting? Juana Cota paced. She talked to her feet as if they were her close confidants. She plopped down next to her son for short moments, but could not settle. An hour passed without relief for any of the three birds. I considered removing the mystery fish. What if it attracted rats that then nibbled on Jack? On the other hand, what if it turned out to be the chick's only menu option for an entire week? I counted the clues and questions in my head.

One: albatross are legends of affection. Mates snuggle for hours on end. They express distress over boundaries and beloveds, but when they get mad, it's usually over quickly. What could cause such sustained dismay in Juana Cota?

Two: Parents are known to rebuke chicks, but it's usually someone else's chick. When young birds beg for feedings from adults other than their own parents, they get nipped. Sometimes they get scolded even if they are entirely innocent. Adults can be cranky about the subject. They search long and far for food and cannot afford to share it with another baby.

Three: Parents do sometimes get a little rough with their own chicks in an effort to get them to beg for food. Did Juana Cota urgently need to feed her son?

Four: Juana Cota and Jose Manuel's last two eggs had failed to hatch. Did she still grieve lost children? Did she sense danger for Monterey Jack? Perhaps she was not yet appeased because it was not apology she sought, nor submission. Perhaps it was safety. But from what? There are no native terrestrial predators in Hawai'i. No coyotes, no eagles, no snakes.

I watched and waited. Ultimately I decided to err on the side of non-interference. I packed up my gear. Just as I was starting to walk down the hill, a final clue was carried on the wind from a short distance away. *Mew.* Wait, what? There were no domestic animals nearby, no homes in easy distance. *Mew.*

I knew Kaua'i had at least fifteen thousand homeless cats that were taking a huge toll on native birdlife. I could not immediately find this specific feline, but I knew he must be an abandoned animal—or the offspring of one—living on whatever he could find. He was likely hungry, perhaps desperate. With that big fish next to Monterey Jack, the chick might as well have had a can of catnip at his feet and overhead speakers chanting *Here kitty kitty.* If I left it in his nest today, tomorrow I wouldn't find Jack. I would find a wing here, a head there, and downy bits everywhere.

I took the fish away. The next day the cat was trapped and taken to the Humane Society.

Case closed.

Three

Fledging

LUKA—MAKANI'S ONE AND ONLY CHICK—thrived in 1979 because a temporary fence protected her. Built by the Young Adult Conservation Corps, it was described in the *'Elepaio,* the Hawai'i Audubon Society newsletter. Unfortunately, the fence was removed after Luka fledged and was "not possible to rebuild" the following nesting season. Because of that, Makani was killed in 1980 when she was attacked by a dog. Exquisitely faithful to her egg, she did not stand a chance against a predator.

We have a few other details about Makani's life: we know she hatched at Midway in 1970 and raised Luka at Kīlauea Point when she was nine years old. We know she was ten when she died. We know Luka was the first documented albatross to fledge from Kaua'i in modern history. These are all recorded facts. From that point, we can only make our best guesses about Luka: whether she was female, when she returned, who her mate was, where they raised their own chicks. Similar guesses must be made for Luka's progeny. To that end, real-life albatross stories have been assigned to each of her possible descendants, stretching from Luka to her great-great-grandchild Kāloakūlua.

Luka returned home when she was four years old and continued to come back each year. She was eight years old when she chose Lopaka for her mate, and he preferred another colony a few miles away from Kīlauea. He was strong and reliable; she was gregarious and inquisitive. It was a good match.

As with many other young breeders, it took them time to learn the mysterious, complex skills of parenting. The first year, when Luka was eight, they couldn't quite synchronize their incubation calendars. How does a mama, five hundred miles out at sea, know when it's her turn? How does a papa prepare for a month-long shift without food or water?

Hatching chick peeps to parent

Alas, although their egg was unprotected only six days out of more than sixty, it was too much exposure. The next year in their second breeding attempt when Luka was nine, her egg inexplicably shattered under her. She and Lopaka stayed with the fragments for several days. They spoke to them. They even seemed to speak to the ants that feasted on the gooey contents.

The third year, when Luka was ten, the couple chose to move to a spot farther into the woods. The site had its own ledge for landings and takeoffs. It had elevation and it had shade. It was perfect. But would this egg fail, like the previous ones?

Over the next nine weeks, Luka and Lopaka regularly touched their bills to the curves of the calcium condo that held their daughter. Hōkūlani stayed curled like a question in her warm wet world until one day the sun spoke her name.

A bird breakout is called *pipping*. For an albatross chick, it can take days. Hōkūlani began uttering tiny peeps inside her shell even before she pricked the first pinhole. She was still a prisoner in a cramped cell, her sounds muffled inside the only chamber she'd ever known. Lopaka returned from fishing, as if he'd heard his baby's voice on the sparkles of the sea, miles away. Her parents were invisible angels, beckoning her to freedom, promising forever. They could have easily broken the egg with a single swift stroke of their mighty bills. They did not. As they waited, perhaps they silently shared the story and the wisdom of their clan.

We are thrilled beyond the stars you are here.
You are from an ancient lineage known as SeaWinders.
Our Mother is the Sea, our Father is the Wind; we hold them Holy.
Our Goddess is the Earth. It is She who gives water to Mother Sea and air to Father Wind. It is She who created our ancestors. It is She who guides us, provides for us, protects us. We are faithful to Her in all we do.
From Mother Sea comes food. Because Mother Sea leads squid to light, we are given sustenance. Because of squid we can fly. Because we can fly we can live.
From Mother Sea comes land. Because of land we can find each other. Because of land we can create new SeaWinders and give them as gifts to Goddess Earth.
From Father Wind comes flight. Because of Father Wind we can fly over Mother Sea. Because of Father Wind we can find land and food and each other.
From Father Wind comes voice. Because of voice we can chant. Because we can chant we can honor Goddess Earth. Because we chant we can be grateful.

Hōkūlani listened—not with her ears, but with her bones—to the silent wisdom from her parents. She summoned all her strength and pecked a tiny hole in her shell. She swallowed daylight for the first time. Luka stood up, bent over, and lightly touched the tip of her bill to her daughter's—the only part of Hōkūlani yet emerged.

They exchanged their first *aloha. Alo* for presence, *ha* for breath.

Is there a greater tenderness in all creation than the moment a mother first lays eyes on her newborn? Hōkūlani rested while Luka continued to silently impart SeaWinder ways.

You are Hōkūlani. You are descended from the great Makani the Wayfinder.
You are the daughter of Luka, who is the daughter of Makani.
Memorize our smells and the patterns in our feathers.
Watch everything that flies on Father Wind.
Everything with wings is your teacher.

Hōkūlani panted. She rested her head against the edge of the hole in her egg and fell asleep. Luka continued.

Cultivate courage and keep it near.
Hunt squid and tolerate hunger.
Make friends with solitude.
There is no such thing
As being alone.

After two days of chipping away at the hole, Hōkūlani enlisted the last of her energy and forced her shoulders to spread her cramped body. Her shell cracked slowly, its fault lines etching erratic patterns. When

Hōkūlani and Lolana

the top half broke, her upper body was free. It was a grand emancipation. She had never before stretched her muscles. She had never before
opened her eyes. When she did, the first thing she saw was her mother's
face. What greater sight is there, in all the heavens?

She collapsed onto Lopaka's feet, spent.

Twelve years later, Hōkūlani and Lolana snuggled under an ironwood
tree. Each new nesting season brought a fleeting opportunity for the
albatross pair to bask in the presence of each other. Their joy was as
strong as the winds that transported them here. They had eyes for no
one and nothing else.

They were both female. Hōkūlani was the daughter of Luka and the
granddaughter of Makani the Wayfinder. Lolana was her devoted mate.
Every year they met at the same spot, give or take a few feet. They met
at the same time, give or take a few days.

This year Hōkūlani was the first one home from sea. She shook herself off. She got reacquainted with the feeling of solid ground under her
feet. She rearranged nesting material, chatted with the other early birds,
and stared out to the horizon until Lolana returned.

They had been successful parents twice before. The previous year they
raised a strong son. When they reunited every November, they spent
hours—sometimes days—nuzzling, napping, and nest building. They
preened. They stared at each other. They were the soft feathers and dark
eyes of a winter romance. The joining, the knowing, the relief.

They had intimate conversations. *Eeh eeh eeh. Eeh eeh eeh eeh.* Were
the lovers renewing their vows? Perhaps they shared newly discovered
fishing latitudes. Maybe they described the exact location of an itch, or
a certain neck ache after so many months in flight. Perhaps they told
riddles and composed poetry.

About a week after their reunion, they each laid an egg in the same
soft concavity. They took turns incubating. Over the next ten days, they
gradually buried one of the eggs in the dirt under the nest, into a dimple excavated by the mothers' sharp toenails and strong bills. One egg

disappeared, one remained. How did they decide which was the chosen one?

Even the chosen one offered no promises. Unless some sperm had squiggled into the picture before the egg was laid, it would not hatch. Either Hōkūlani or Lolana would need to have gotten a donation from an acceptable boy. Coitus would have been over quickly. Albatross males are typically devoted to every stage, but in this case a donor was unlikely to have helped the females during the rigors of brooding and chick rearing. His sole duty would have been over.

Alas, even the chosen one failed to hatch. Perhaps the mamas hadn't found someone suitable. Perhaps they had found someone suitable, but he did not have the sexual expertise to line up their personal parts, cloaca-to-cloaca. Perhaps they had waited for one particular guy with great genes and temperament—the previous papa maybe—but he never materialized.

The chosen one got all the same devotion a fertile egg would have gotten. Hōkūlani and Lolana were steadfast and diligent. You really had to wonder what they knew. As veteran parents, couldn't they sense the absence of a growing chick? Maybe yes, maybe no. Still, they each took long shifts on the nest. When hatch failed at sixty-two days, the usual incubation period, they waited. When it still failed at seventy-two days, they waited. When it failed by eighty-two days, they waited. They waited eighty-eight days, which amounted to twenty-six days of overtime.

Their profound patience reminded me of a man I met in India several years ago. I was in a rural area north of Mumbai as a volunteer nurse for an "eye camp," where villagers went to have their cataracts surgically removed. They were Adivasi, the aboriginal people of India, and among the poorest of the poor. They lived in huts; entire households subsisted on the equivalent of two dollars a day. Their cataracts had rendered them almost completely blind, which had made them burdensome to their families. All surgical candidates had arrived with escorts so they could find their way around.

The eye camp was chaotic. People came and went constantly. The daytime temperature hovered around one hundred ten degrees. I was assigned the job of day-shift charge nurse for a tent that held about three hundred beds, or roughly ten times the number of beds an American charge nurse would oversee. In reality, the "beds" were padded mats laid out in parallel lines on the tent floor. At both ends of the tent were enormous fans with only one speed: hurricane. I was supposed to be doing preoperative intakes, but it was difficult to know which patient was which. We had only one translator in our tent, and I knew only one word in the patients' language: *pani*. Water. Many of the patients knew one word in English: *sister*. Nurse.

On the first day of surgery, a man was sent back from the operating room without having had his cataracts removed. I never knew the reason. He was sent back again on the second day. He sat waiting at the foot of his mat, overtly patient and unworried. Whenever I walked past him, his escort nudged him and he smiled, bowed his head in my direction, put his hands together in prayer, and said, "Namaste, sister."

The third time his surgery was postponed, I asked the translator to tell him how sorry I was he had to wait so long. "It must be frustrating," I said therapeutically.

"Sister, mention not," he said through the translator. "What is waiting?" he asked. "Soon I will see again. Seeing is everything."

One day in late February, Hōkūlani and Lolana decided it was time to stop waiting. They walked away and stood on the bluff, then returned to check their nest once again. They talked to each other. They stretched. Finally a combination of wind, hunger, and surrender set them free. Perhaps the chosen one's silence reassured them. Perhaps the other egg, the long-buried one, added further depth to the truth.

Perhaps they were actually free all along. Perhaps Hōkūlani and Lolana took turns with the chosen one for eighty-eight days for other reasons. Perhaps they stayed for each other, for the brief company they got when they traded places, for the love of it. Because they loved each other, and because they loved even the idea of another baby. Is not the notion of a blessing also a blessing?

When the two mamas flew from the bluff, they flew separately. They were unlikely to see each other again for nearly nine months.

Squid willing, next November they will meet at the same spot, give or take a few feet.

They will meet at the same time, give or take a few days.

They will have eyes for no one and nothing else. They will lay two eggs.

Hōkūlani and Lolana did indeed have a fertile egg the following season. She was Luka's granddaughter and Makani the Wayfinder's great-granddaughter. Her name was Kaluahine, named after the area where she hatched.

Like all albatross chicks under heaven, she had very limited face-to-face time with her parents. When she was blonde-tipped and five days old, one of her two moms was there around the clock. When she was five weeks old, she got brief visits every few days. When she was five months old, she had forged a full-time friendship with solitude. At that age she retained her cool punky look but was practically an adult—except where an empty stomach was concerned. There, she was still utterly dependent upon her parents. That would change, of course, the moment she flew. But now she craved a meal. She was famished.

It was her lucky day. She saw a shadow glide up the hillside, heading fast in her direction. Kaluahine jumped up and read the feather pattern under the bird's wings. It was her mama Lolana! The chick peeped herself into a frenzy, ecstatic for the delivery of a certain cephalopod, for the feel of a full belly, for the comfort of familial conversation. Her mom did not disappoint. After a hearty meal, yet another bird appeared from the north. She bypassed the bluff, banked perpendicular to the earth, and skidded to a landing. It was her other mama! It was Hōkūlani! Lolana was thrilled too, and displayed her excitement by puffing up her chest and speaking to her feet. Her beloved trotted toward her, equally titillated.

Kaluahine could not remember when she had last seen her mamas together. When they hunkered down, she squatted beside them. She listened to them trade sweet nothings. She added her own quiet chirps to their dialogue. She rested in the serenity of their unmistakable smells and the satiation of her appetite.

Then, at a moment when Hōkūlani was scratching Lolana's perfect itch, Kaluahine made a bold choice: she leaned forward and tenderly preened Hōkūlani's neck. Before that act, she had always been the recipient, the one preened. For the first time, Kaluahine was preening someone other than herself. She asked for nothing. There was no plea, no urgency, no plan. Her gesture may have been small but the gift was cosmic. You could call it mimicry, you could call it rehearsal, you could call it bonding. You could call it gratitude; you could call it aloha. Whatever you call it, it was a perceptual shift worthy of "Pomp and Circumstance."

What is love if not a graduation from one consciousness into another?

At five months old, Kaluahine was no longer the center of the universe. Her mothers would soon be gone. She did not know when—or if—she would see them again.

She was a big girl now.

Although the process of banding albatross chicks is quick, it always looms larger in my mind than the time it takes to execute. On a prearranged day, wildlife agency professionals rendezvous with citizen scientists. Together we access colonies on private properties. One by one, a loose ring is placed on each leg of the newly feathered babes, making them forevermore identifiable as individuals.

I had visited colonies once or twice a week throughout the season. I knew Kaluahine's personality and her curious popularity among unrelated adults. I knew her moms, Hōkūlani and Lolana. I knew how hard they worked to raise her. I knew Kaluahine had no experience with human clusters. She had never seen more than two people at one time; most days she saw no people at all. She didn't know how we smelled up close. She had never heard our outside voices. She had never learned to be on guard. One cloudy morning she suddenly found herself encircled by humans—an event that could not have made any sense to her—so she summoned her only defenses. She clapped her bill and tried to back up. She made gagging sounds. I snatched her into my arms and positioned her head skyward. She kicked and struggled. I held her close to keep her wings and airway safe. I didn't care about getting puked on; I cared about the precious contents of her stomach. We didn't want her to aspirate, nor did we want her to lose a single ounce of food. Her most recent meal likely cost her parents thousands of miles of pelagic foraging.

A biologist clamped on two painless rings—one metal ring with tiny engraved numbers and one black plastic ring with large white numbers. Two small white feathers were plucked from under the brown fluff on her chest. They were sealed in a bag and labeled.

During the time I held Kaluahine, my ear was close to her face. She cried an almost inaudible whimper, a sigh accompanied by a wheeze. There was discomfort in her voice, and what seemed like an attempt to communicate. For a big bird whose body is filled with sacs of air, a human hug must feel like suffocation. Panic, bondage, treason. Betrayal.

I disliked playing the part of Benedict Arnold. On banding days I had no choice. I wanted to bolt from Ben's presence, but I did not. No. I stayed, despite the stench of him. I did the job.

What's indispensable sometimes trumps what's intolerable.

I whispered my apologies into Kaluahine's neck. I drew in the subtle musk of her down. I inhaled stardust and the origins of the sea. I remembered a haunting song from long ago, from Camp Fire Girls: "Where Does the Wind Come From?" I felt guilty about how Kaluahine's smells filled me with such pleasure.

I've read about people who get a thrill from the act of putting a ring on a bird. To them it's evidently like putting a ring on a lover. Each bird then wears a token of the bander, which in turn allows a piece of the human to go wild. It allows people to send a message into the future and imagine themselves hearing back, informing them where their beloved has been. By going places people cannot, the birds are said to expand human horizons.

It made me ache to hear Kaluahine's resignation, to know her fear. She reminded me of one of my goddaughters. When Maile was in middle school, her parents cooked meals in an indoor-outdoor kitchen in a rural valley on Kaua'i. Maile was braver than most adults. She surfed big waves and trekked the Himalayas. But cute little geckos? The harmless reptiles freaked her out. Worse, they were all over the place. It was common for six or eight of them to hang out on the ceiling, above the kitchen table, catching insects and chirping like baby birds.

One night during dinner a gecko fell from the ceiling onto Maile's lap. She screamed and ran to her room, inconsolable. I followed her. She was so miserable, I wept just to see her face.

"Don't cry, Auntie," she said, a child of compassion. She smiled sweetly at my uselessness. I told her I wasn't crying to make her stop. I wasn't crying to influence anything. I was crying because it made me grieve to see her so distressed. I was crying because I couldn't accept my inability to protect her from panic.

Nor, in that moment, could I accept Kaluahine being threaded through the eye of the needle of human perception. After banding, for better or for worse, from that day forward, even if she forgot the whole event, Kaluahine would forever be woven into a foreign tapestry. It was not a fabric she would have chosen.

Kaluahine was in my arms for a few short minutes. When the job was done I bent down, placed her feet on the ground and released her. For a moment she leaned on my leg like a sleepy puppy. When she attempted to walk away, she stumbled. Had I stolen her equilibrium along with her innocence? In the end, I'm sure it hurt me more than it hurt her. At least I hope that's the truth.

If they survive, Kaluahine and her classmates will return to this colony in a few years. Because of banding we will recognize them. We will have data about the gender and age of the birds, their home island, and who

Kaluakane and Kaluahine

mated with whom. Because of data we can help them. Because of data we can create additional safe habitat. Without banding we cannot know one bird from another. Without banding I cannot tell you these stories.

Eleven years after the banding, Kaluahine, great-granddaughter of Makani the Wayfinder, got a call from home. So did Kaluakane, her handsome mate. No matter how many thousands of miles away they were, no matter where they were on the winds of the North Pacific, in the Bering Sea or the Gulf of Alaska, they got the message.

"Come home, honey," the call said. "It's time for love."

The birds didn't hesitate. Would you? They hadn't seen each other in months. They turned on a dime and headed south. As usual, the males were the first to arrive. They waited. Some napped in the forest like icons of feathered serenity. Kaluakane stood solitary, facing the ocean like a sentinel. One set of males clustered in the woods close to a cliff.

At first the little circle appeared friendly, as if the guys were swapping swashbuckling squid stories. But things got touchy fast. They started snapping at each other over imaginary trespasses. They squealed and pulled tail feathers, then acted like they had no alternative but to tolerate such annoying proximity. It's amateur victim stuff, devoid of bloodshed but lousy with feigned innocence. You could roll your eyes at the drama, you really could.

The males had acres to choose from. But rather than squatting a good chunk of land or claiming a specific nest site, these guys squeezed into square footage the size of a queen-sized mattress. I felt like reminding them of their stellar reputations. *Dudes, seriously? Aren't you supposed to be the easy-going sojourners of the high seas?* Not that they would have listened. They had only one thing on their minds. Fortunately for all concerned, the girls started arriving right on schedule.

Kaluahine and Kaluakane reunited and were instantly hot for each other. Sex, however, is not as simple as it might seem to the human eye. For one thing, albatross have precious little practice in the art of perching. You never see one sitting in a tree or on a telephone pole. Kaluakane had to pick a route to climb aboard his ladylove. When he tried to access her from the front end, he found himself pointing the wrong direction once he got on top. He had to dismount—okay, fall off—and try again. Once he climbed back up and was facing the same direction as Kaluahine, he had to stretch his wings to stay balanced like a tightrope walker on a high wire. With one webbed foot on each of her shoulders, his posture required focused concentration.

Kaluahine also had to accept his mount. She was accustomed to wind, not bulk, on her back. He weighed eight pounds; she weighed seven. She had to stay completely still, like a Ukrainian gymnast, regulating her breath and supporting him. She also had to get her tail out of the way to allow him access to his desired destination. He pressed his tail down and to the right. She lifted hers to the left. He rocked his pelvis. The males of most bird species do not have penises; there is no penetration. The goal is a *cloacal kiss*, the merging of two pink private parts that resemble pencil erasers. When the erasers do actually touch, his sperm

Kaluahine with little Kāloakūlua

has to be ready, like *NOW, dude!* He kept on thrusting for as long as he was able to maintain his equilibrium and she was able to support his weight.

Ultimately, however, humping got trumped by breathing. Kaluahine had no choice but to stand up, and Kaluakane had no choice but to jump off.

It was truly an act of athletic artistry, a regular cirque du seabird. When it was over (in this case, thirty-seven seconds) they stayed together overnight, making out under a tree, scratching every last itch. Albatross love can go on for days. What other species spends so much time in pre- and post-passion affection? Wolves come to mind. Who else? Certainly not dogs or cats. When it comes to sex, domestic pets do not pet.

Back at the colony, our lovers had the opportunity to tarry at least in part because of their well-chosen necking spot. Since they were in a fairly protected place, they were unlikely to have dogs or pigs barge in on their intimate moments. But Kaluahine and Kaluakane were not thinking about predators. For them, "mate for life" meant they got about two weeks a year together. They savored it. The hard work would start soon enough. Tomorrow, to be exact.

Kaluahine and Kaluakane had a daughter named Kāloakūlua. She was named for the phase of the moon when she began to pip from the shell, the phase when she took her first breath. She was a little girl with a big destiny. Kāloakūlua turned out to be the star player of a reality show, and instantly became the most-watched albatross in the world. As the great-great-granddaughter of Makani the Wayfinder, she had heroism in her genes. From the moment she hatched in a winter deluge until the much-anticipated moment she fledged in the summer sunshine, the lens of a camera from the Cornell Lab of Ornithology followed her, dawn to dusk. Every poop, preen, and perambulation was live-streamed from the island of Kaua'i to anyone on the globe with sufficient interest and bandwidth. In the first five months, Kāloakūlua logged nearly two million hits from viewers in one hundred and ninety-five countries. Talk about an ambassador.

Sometimes our leading lady's style was considered by biologists to be standard for her species; some behaviors had never been previously observed or tested. Who knew, for example, how she would relate to a rooster at a human wedding?

Expel guano with grace. Kāloakūlua never fouled her immediate environs. Even when she was wet and exhausted from the rigors of pipping, she wiggled to the edge of the nest, lifted her tiny bottom, and lobbed her guano in an arc like a three-point basketball shot from half-court. Cleanliness is next to albatrossliness.

Have your home and chew it too. For two months, Kāloakūlua lived inside an egg and was created by its contents. After she emerged, she snacked on her shell. She lived in dirt and picked up things off the ground like any self-respecting toddler. Later she lived on a lawn. She mouthed grass like a cow and tossed it like a golfer, exploring her tastes and talents. Her ultimate address—the wind—she would gulp with abandon.

Make unexpected connections. Kāloakūlua's downy warmth allowed her parents to leave her unattended when she was only three weeks old. In their absence, she found herself in close proximity to at least one species of mollusk, three species of mammals, and a dozen species of birds. Red-crested cardinals, chestnut mannikins, and ruddy turnstones poked in the ground within a few inches of her. *Nēnē*—Hawaiian geese—grazed in the grass. She watched them, focused and curious. She objected to none of them. A wild rooster named George, about the same age as Kāloakūlua, became her buddy. He napped near her nest, bobbed with courting albatross adults, and just hung out. Who could guess the content of communication between a chicken and a 'tross? Whatever information Kāloakūlua and George may or may not have exchanged, they seemed to take pleasure in each other's company.

When the time is right, move. Kāloakūlua checked out of her original leaf-dirt-ironwood nest when she was a few weeks old, like it was a hotel. She then built a new nest of weeds and grass clippings about fifteen feet away. That was home base for a couple of months. Then she moved to a spot under a palm tree. For two nights she lived next to a driveway and scared the guano out of the TrossCam operators. After that she relocated to a spot closer to her runway on the bluff.

Practice the patience of a pine. Like all albatross chicks, she spent days and weeks waiting for supper. Since she ate seafood exclusively, she could not get nutrition from seeds, grass, or insects like the other birds in the vicinity. Even though she was bright and inquisitive, she never seemed distressed by boredom. She watched, she wondered, she wandered.

Look for UFOs. Kāloakūlua was an only child who knew how to keep herself entertained. Everything that flew was an object of interest, even though some were fairly foreign to her species: bees, butterflies, mynas fighting over bananas ten feet above her head, frigate birds chasing red-footed boobies, ultralight aircraft, tourist helicopters. You name it. If it moved overhead, the chick was a fan.

Do improv. Comedy improv is rendered from "yes, and" reactions. Example: let's say you're in a long, slow line at the grocery store. The stranger in front of you smiles. "It could be worse," she says. You smile back and gesture to the cover of a gossip magazine featuring the cellulite of celebrity X. You say (yes, and), "We could have paparazzi chasing us." She says (yes, and), "Oh look, Dolly Parton has a secret girlfriend in Georgia." The lady behind you chimes in (yes, and), "Seriously? Who knew Dolly could speak Russian?" Bingo. You leave the store unperturbed. Why? Like Kāloakūlua, you didn't waste all your energy resisting reality.

Our starlet had countless experiences that 99 percent of albatross have never had, including: lawn mowers with shirtless drivers, red-crested cardinals with strong reactions to their own reflection in a certain lens, ragged feral cats, cruise ships at sunset, tree trimmers rocking to reggae, blue beach balls bouncing from a playful child's hands, and a green blender-sized camera hanging on a post. All events were met without the slightest hint of fear. When dozens of guests showed up for a wedding, she did not hide. No. She waddled *toward* the cars that brought the guests.

Be a verb. As mentioned, *kāloakūlua* refers to the phase of the moon when our star took her first breath of air. A moon phase sounds like a noun but acts like a verb. It's defined by a moving shadow as much as the presence of a moving rock. A noun freezes time and pretends it's the big cheese. A verb—not unlike Kāloakūlua—inhales, expels, knows, moves, looks, practices, pukes, gives, and lives.

Give the 'do its due. Albatross feathers tend to appear on the torso first. The closer Kāloakūlua got to first flight, the more she looked like an adult from the neck down. The top of the head was where the distinctions among the chicks got really entertaining. Appearance options included biker dude, babushka, Einstein, Eddie Izzard, comb-over, Morticia, Friar Tuck, Miley Cyrus, Bozo the Clown, Billy Idol, and Barbra Streisand. In the last few weeks before she fledged, Kāloakūlua wore a downy lei around her neck, then had a silly unibrow, then—as the last bits of fuzz fell off—she had a dot in the middle of her forehead like a Hindu convert.

Puke the sharp stuff. When possible, mōlī hurl things they cannot digest. When it comes to plastics, adult albatross do far better than chicks. They all get rid of squid beaks, those black switchblade-sharp, shiny things. There's a metaphor here somewhere. Why hold on to rubbish and pain?

Live long and trossper. There are so very many things that could have gone wrong for Kāloakūlua. As an egg she might have been laid someplace more dangerous, near a colony of homeless cats or in an open field frequented by hunting dogs. The egg could have been infertile. Her parents might have underestimated how much attention their egg needed or gotten their wires crossed about whose turn it was to incubate it. After she hatched, she might have been fed too little food or too much plastic. Predators could have killed her. Avian pox on her eye could have blinded her. Her parents could have drowned on fishhooks. She might have crawled under a car during the wedding. There might not have been property owners who cared. There might not have been a reliable power source or the technology to stream her face like a Cupid's arrow straight to millions of human hearts. There might not have been people willing to donate money for equipment. There might not have been women who volunteered hundreds of cam-op hours for one hundred and fifty days.

So many things could have gone wrong, but they didn't.

Kāloakūlua must have had a mighty fine celestial bodyguard. Maybe more than one. Maybe she was surrounded by an entire heavenly host, a full-time flock of angels and archangels, guides and guardians, saints and siddhas. Seraphim above her head and cherubim at her side.

Her divine protection was never more palpable than on a certain Friday in April. She was sixty-seven days old, not even yet midway between hatch and fledge.

It was the day she met Makakilo.

More accurately, it was the day Makakilo met her.

It was 6:30 a.m. when I heard the buzz of my cell phone. I braced myself when I saw it was Susan, one of the TrossCam volunteers. "A friend just called from Seattle," she said. "There's a dog on the cam."

"What? When?" I asked, as if the reply mattered. My heart raced. I pushed away from my desk. I had seen way too many dog-killed albatross over the years, and it was hard to imagine how a defenseless ground-nesting baby bird could survive an unleashed canine visitor. "A couple minutes ago," she said. "How far away?" I asked. Data can be such empty comfort. There is no such thing as a safe distance. "Right by the nest," she said. She told me Kāloakūlua didn't look injured, but she couldn't tell for sure. The chick was not moving.

"I'll call when I get there," I said. I zipped up my hiking pants and threw on a fleece top. I fumbled with my car keys. As the garage door opened, I called for reinforcements. I was only fifteen minutes away, but Nicki lived even closer. She picked up right away.

"There's a dog," I said, backing my car into the driveway. "Are you sure?" she asked. She already knew the answer. She was just as alarmed as I was. "I'm right behind you," Nicki said. She had to feed her bed and breakfast customers first. She decided they'd be happy with cold fruit and hot muffins.

We wanted magic. We bargained for refuge, a ray of hope that we had misunderstood something fundamental or someone was simply wrong. We wanted the dog to be an apparition or a nightmare. We asked who, what, when, where as if we were on assignment for the *New York Times*. We wanted the event to already be in the past, over and done, with a good outcome. Or in the future, like next year. Or next century. Mostly we wanted it to be never. Who doesn't want to postpone a broken heart?

It was nine miles to the nest. In the first mile, my brain scrambled. It allowed strange recollections across the threshold into consciousness, including a bad television commercial I saw once and thought I had forgotten. Where do these things come from? Here's how the ad went:

"What are the five words a woman never wants to hear?" a man's somber voice asked.

Good God, I thought, there were so many possibilities. Why would I want to conjure up any of them?

"I can see your foundation," the voice gravely answered.

Wait, what? Are you out of your mind? I confess I do not have enough girly genes to fully understand what the commercial meant. My idea of makeup is lip balm SPF forty-five. If I had to choose from a thousand five-word sentences competing in a bad news contest, "I can see your foundation" would never qualify as a contestant. "A dog's at the nest," on the other hand, would be way up there. Five words straight from the depths of hell.

In the third mile, I struggled harder to control the horrific images metastasizing to every part of my body. I prayed and I chanted. I called on 'aumākua and ancestors, both human and feathered. I summoned angels. I brazenly called on Hawaiian gods, Catholic martyrs, and Hindu deities. I called on the patron saints of albatross, hunting dogs, owners of hunting dogs, builders of humane traps, donors to humane societies, owners of private property, banks that give loans to private property owners. Who else? I couldn't bear to think of Kāloakūlua hurt.

In the seventh mile, I remembered I should call on the district—the *moku*—of Kaua'i, but realized I didn't know which ancient chiefdom the nest was in. Halele'a? Ko'olau? Why didn't I know that? At the ninth mile I turned off the highway onto a short road that headed *makai*, toward the sea. I imagined posting good news on Twitter. At the end of the road, I opened a gate into a driveway. I was about fifty yards away from the nest, then thirty, then twenty. So far no dog.

I parked. I walked toward the cam. Kāloakūlua looked like a lump of brown fur. She was just a nine-week-old baby, innocent and adorable. "Hey you," I said, standing about fifteen feet away. She didn't move. Was she breathing? Was I? I moved closer. Wait, did I see her chest rise? Yes! She was alive! Like any nurse I mentally assessed her condition. I saw no blood, no vomit, no dog saliva on her neck. Her wings were connected to her torso. Was it possible she was unhurt? Her head popped up. She yawned and preened herself. She didn't seem to notice me.

Nicki arrived with muffins. Everyone watching the cam could now see Kāloakūlua was unharmed. My cell phone became a communication hub. Texts and tweets flew. Thomas, the property manager, gave us unlimited access to keep the chick safe. Charles at Cornell turned off the public audio so we could problem-solve on site. Hollie posted a photo of the dog's distinct markings. Susan arrived with a huge pig trap that took four people to unload. Jeanine arrived with dog food, leashes, and pizza. A nearby vet offered to loan us a tranquilizer gun, so Nicki retrieved it. Penny at the Humane Society advised us not to use the gun, so Nicki returned it. Marcia brought a dog carrier. Stuart rigged the pig trap so it would stop slamming shut in gusts of wind. Mana arrived with a second trap so we could cover both ingress routes. Seabird biologists Beth and Lindsay gave us vital counsel. Barb and Jody covered TrossCam duties.

As we watched the video replay, we all felt indebted to the dog, for how he sniffed Kāloakūlua's neck and inexplicably walked away. We commented on the beauty of his blue eyes. Mika named him Makakilo for his ability to see deeply, for his powers of observation.

For three days we took shifts standing guard. After two weeks the traps had only been visited by wild chickens with an appetite for raw beef ribs. Makakilo was never seen near the nest again, but remained homeless and hungry for another month. He was ultimately caught, ragged and thin, at a nearby ginger farm. The Kaua'i Humane Society picked him up. He was fed and bathed and exercised. He was put up for adoption. Weeks went by. Kim posted a story on Facebook and a local family chose him. He got a real home.

Although I am uncertain of the process by which official status is conferred, you may consider this my nomination for St. Makakilo. What is sainthood if not gentle behavior with holy help?

Please pass the wine.

If hunger conjured courage, Kāloakūlua was brave. It was time to jump off the cliff and fly. The albatross chicks in their separate colonies tackled the truth differently, each according to his or her constitution, growth, and personality. One tucked his neck into his shoulders, saved his energy, napped. One hopped all over the place like a high school cheerleader recruiting fans. Did she advocate a group plunge? One turned his back and stared toward the mountains, as if ignoring the ledge would make it go away. One spread her wings beatifically, closed her eyes to the sun, and prepared to be summoned forth.

One chick spotted his mother coming in from sea. He had not eaten in ten days, and the chick seemed startled at his good fortune. He ran toward her. He rattled his bill against hers like a swordsman, begging. Another chick tried to share in the bounty, but was soundly scolded. She waddled away and genuflected before the cheerleader.

Kāloakūlua's most recent fast had lasted fourteen days. When the trade winds were strong, she ran toward them, got some lift, landed on her feet. She trotted back to the start of her grassy runway, peeping all the while, and tried again. Then hark! In the middle of flight practice her father, Kaluakane, arrived with flying fish from the firmament. Kaluakane offered his daughter a hardy buffet and a heroic buffer. Like a protective dad of an adventuresome adolescent, he chased away Mango, the only other chick on the bluff. Not that his little girl needed

Mango goes goofyfoot.

it. Recently Kāloakūlua had run off Mango more than the other way around. She was tough and tender, brazen and funny. In Hawai'i she would be known as a *tita*.

After a long snooze in the afternoon of the summer solstice, papa Kaluakane walked over to check on his girl. He seemed wholly satisfied with what he saw. She lifted her eyes and memorized him one last time. On her neck, wisps of down fluttered and furled in the breeze. In the morning he was gone. Although land was the only home his daughter had ever known, twenty-four hours later she could no longer resist the powerful pull to the Pacific. She hopped onto a rock wall, pumped her wings and in one leap, changed her address to a zip code called *wind*.

E mālama pono, Kāloakūlua. Take care.

It was a big moment in Mango's life too. He had nailed ground school. Now he too had to gather the guts to actually take off. There were no instructors, no copilots, no practice flights. When he flew, it would be for good. Solo. It was a great day for it. There was a fine wind, his feathers were full, and his muscles were strong. Did he hesitate, just a little? You couldn't blame him if he did. His supple feet had never left the ground, unless you count the lift he got from hopping. As long as he kept his webs planted on terra firma, he didn't have to deal with challenges like crashing into the sea, encountering sharks, or foraging for squid.

He stood on the summit of a little hillock just uphill from where he hatched one hundred and fifty-four days ago. He was a bright boy, no doubt about it. When he was only four weeks old, he left his first nest and climbed to a new spot under a mango tree. It became his namesake. He plucked all the weeds in the radius of his reach and built himself a cozy new bed between the exposed roots. It was a clever relocation for a young bird with a downy coat living in a tropical climate where shade was a definite plus.

His internal GPS had been forever programmed to this exact mound. He knew it well, its sights and scents and sounds. He knew its elevation and how much speed he could get from a running descent. He knew how to crest the knoll and navigate its circumference. Unless one of his parents was around, he was king of the hill. He hung out with cattle egrets, nēnē geese, and jungle fowl. He slept right through the noise of lawn mowers and weed whackers. His one conflict was the harmless border dispute he had with Kāloakūlua. The two birds always managed to settle their beefs without bloodshed. Because of his clan's unparalleled aptitude, Mango was on the cusp of joining all other albatross as the world's most magnificent long-distance flyers.

But not right that moment. Right that moment the wind was his flight simulator; he stood still and rode it like a wave. See him stand, face the nose, and strike the pose! See him lift his wings like sails! See him stare fearlessly into the face of destiny! He led with his right leg, a stance surfers call *goofyfoot*. His airborne identity waited in the literal wings, eager to overthrow the old earthbound regime, to mutiny against gravity; still, Mango held on. He took one last great ride. He had "Good Vibrations" in an *Endless Summer*.

Mango and infinity pool

Northeasterly breezes blew the down on his head and gave him a slapstick look. What did he care if his hairstyle looked like one of the Three Stooges? He was a bad dude. The surf was pumping, epic, gnarly. He was in the pocket, the most powerful part of a wave, right before it breaks. He felt the rush of his body's acceleration even though he was standing perfectly still, going nowhere fast. He was flying without flying. He stood in the dead center between push and pull, stay and go, land and sea, life and death, here and there, now and never. Between Look Before You Leap and He Who Hesitates Is Lost.

At 154 days old, flight was still a dream for Mango. The next day it would become a reality. As it turned out, 155 days old was the perfect age to fledge.

No one would have believed how he did it.

It was time for Mango's commencement. Learning to fly is always a big deal, but here's the thing: Not one single albatross has ever fledged the way he fledged. Not ever, not anywhere, not once since feathers began.

He wasn't used to being the star. For the first two-thirds of his life, Mango played the supporting role in the mōlī reality show. While he was behind the scenes, the leading lady was followed by a remote-control camera that hung from a low post, silently streaming bits of Kāloakūlua's early life into a narrative for the ages. Anyone with computer access could be smitten: from home or a hospital bed or a classroom, from Georgia or Gabon or grandma's garage. Anyone could see Kāloakūlua was drop-dead adorable. She had those big innocent eyes, those stubby wings, that squeezable body. She was everything people love in a baby animal, the stuff of stuffies. Mango was just as appealing, but viewers missed his cutest phase because of simple geography. He was never a secret. His nest just happened to be hidden from view behind a little knoll. Off camera, out of sight, mostly out of mind.

Mango's potential for fame changed when both chicks built their first independent nests. Mango shifted from his original sunny site in a grassy field to the shade of a fruit tree. Kāloakūlua went the opposite direction. She relocated from under her little palm tree and entered broad daylight. As Mango became even more hidden, Kāloakūlua got more visible.

Those moves made a big difference in their social lives, camera or no camera. As visible as she was, Kāloakūlua became a real-deal chick magnet to young adult birds. They could easily spot her as they flew overhead and were drawn to her. Perhaps she triggered in them a passionate desire to make babies. The teens practiced brooding and courting until they were exhausted, all in proximity of a fascinated Kāloakūlua.

For more than three months Mango remained mostly unseen on the far side of the knoll. Then suddenly, when he was ninety-nine days old, he appeared. One minute he was in the wings, as usual, out of sight. The next minute there he was, at the top of the hill, surveying his kingdom. He had grown to be a big boy in those ninety-nine mysterious days. His head and upper torso were still thick with down. He looked like he was wearing a shawl woven from yak fur. It gave him a goofy, earnest look, like he had accidentally stumbled into the tropics from the plateaus of Tibet.

Kāloakūlua saw him too. She was riveted, excited, and a bit hesitant. Did she have an inkling he'd been there all along, just outside her visual field? She must have seen his parents come and go, must have heard him begging for food. Imagine you're an only child and one day you wake up to discover there's another kid who's been living in your house all along. What do you say?

Kāloakūlua chirped. Mango looked back at her, then stood taller. His torso was larger than hers, even though he was a few days younger. Kāloakūlua decided it was time they met. She started to climb Mango's mound. Who knew how he would react?

Although Kāloakūlua seemed interested in making his acquaintance, Mango evidently had a different goal in mind. Maybe he was intimidated by her popularity. Maybe he was a bit cocky about his higher altitude. Maybe he didn't want anyone violating his personal space. Most likely he wanted to be certain there were no interlopers on his turf when one of his parents arrived with a sumptuous meal.

He watched as she got closer and closer until she stepped across a border for which he had no intention of issuing a visa. She sensed his displeasure and stopped. He ran straight at her. Just before he got there, he tripped. He righted himself and tossed a few squeals in her direction. Both chicks snapped their bills. There was no pain, no bloodshed, no physical contact at all.

She retreated. He almost went after her, and then decided against it. What would be the point? He had made his presence known. He had planted a sovereign flag. She had recognized his nation. Or so it seemed.

When TrossCam viewers realized beloved Kāloakūlua was not even a little hurt, the relationship between the two birds became a source of daily entertainment. A good thing it was, too, because there would be weeks of property claims and dominance discussions between the birds. He marched into her turf, nibbled from her original nest, and challenged her dominion. She mounted his hill from every approach, preferably when he was napping. He petitioned for an easement to the bluff. They engineered new tactics, both bold and sly, to assist their frequent trespasses. Once, in the middle of a forced retreat, Mango stopped, shifted into reverse, waved his fanny in the air, and shot an arc of guano in her direction. It's hard to imagine a more eloquent sentiment.

In the last week before she fledged, Kāloakūlua managed to maintain control over the runway they both needed for flight practice. She had gotten more assertive and was even able to chase off a small flock of nēnē geese. After she flew, Mango had the place to himself for thirteen days. No square footage to conquer, no foot fouls, no line disputes.

Our boy was destined to go out with a bang. He had practiced; he was prepared. But when he could no longer resist the smells of the sea, when the moment came, he miscalculated his takeoff. Instead of getting the lift he anticipated, he splashed down. Not into the sea, but into a human swimming pool. If he had wanted, he could have climbed out, shaken it off, and returned to the runway. But no, he tried something far more daring, something he had never attempted. From the water's surface he started flapping his wings as hard as he could. What did he think he was, a dove? Albatross are not good at taking off vertically. At first he got nowhere. He kept flapping. Still nothing. Then all of a sudden he got enough air to rise out of the pool. Within moments he was a tiny dot on the northern horizon of the great Pacific Ocean.

That monumental feat won Mango the honor of being the first albatross in the history of the good green earth—and perhaps the first bird of any species in millions of years of flight—to fledge from an infinity swimming pool. Talk about deserving a standing ovation. Not bad for a supporting actor who spent the first two-thirds of his life in anonymity.

Let's face it; there were really two celebrities in that reality show. We just didn't know it until the last minute. Literally.

Lisa, one of my goddaughters, had been religiously watching the TrossCam—along with her ten-year-old son Jack—on her laptop at home. One day after work, she and Jack stopped to pick up something for supper and were headed back to their car in the parking lot. As Lisa opened the door, she noticed something on the asphalt. Her chest constricted; her heart pounded. It was a baby bird. She picked it up.

She saw fuzzy feathers, mottled skin, and transparent eyelids. It peeped, breathing fast.

Lisa was torn. She didn't have the wherewithal for another dependent, but she was the kind of mother who put her money where her morals were. At forty-one, she was a model of empathy. She texted me to ask if human odor could cause parental rejection. I told her it was a myth, and that it was best to put the baby back in the nest. Lisa couldn't find it. She decided to help, come hell or high water. The bird was only borderline cute, but to Jack he was Moses in a basket. He cupped the chick in his palms. On the drive home, he informed Lisa the baby's name was Olaf. "Awesome," she said, agreeing the bird totally looked like the snowman in *Frozen*.

Jack ran to get a shoebox from his closet. Lisa emptied his Legos, replaced them with a hand towel, and put the box under a lamp. The boy wondered if Olaf liked Captain Crunch. Lisa texted me again. What could he eat? She mixed an egg with breadcrumbs and rinsed out a Tylenol dropper. Maybe it wasn't a good thing that Jack touched Olaf so often, but Lisa couldn't bear to scold his tenderness. Hadn't there been enough heartbreak already? Later, after they went to bed, Lisa listened to Olaf's squeaky chirps into the night. She finally fell asleep. She had no idea what time it was when Jack woke her up.

"Mommy, I can't hear Olaf." He beseeched her to try Lucky Charms.

Neither hell nor high water had bothered to knock—they simply broke into the apartment and forced Lisa to be braver than she really felt. If Olaf was dead (hell), she would have to figure out how to soften the blow. If he wasn't dead (high water), she would have to figure out how to keep him alive. She remembered that there was no precipice more perilous than her feelings for a baby animal. The issue wasn't its charm and vulnerability. The issue wasn't its need for Lisa. The issue was her utter fatigue of failed relationships. She loved being in love. Who doesn't? But every time she'd been in love, she'd had a bad tendency to say yes to everything. She'd forget how to say no. She'd underestimate consequences. It had been a problem. It was still a problem.

It was even more complicated when the baby animal was wild. The little darlings were hauntingly appealing to Lisa's spirit. She wanted to rescue them, protect them, nurture them. She wanted to be like Androcles in the fable. She believed in the reciprocal nature of mercy. She tried to forget the rest of the story—the part where Androcles put a leash on the lion after he removed that thorn from the big cat's paw. She didn't stop to imagine how the leash worked out for the king of beasts.

After Olaf died, Lisa had a new dilemma. It was Kāloakūlua. She and Jack had both been instantly smitten the first time they watched the little albatross on Lisa's computer. Lisa's adoration was matched only by her vigilance; she became a helicopter auntie. Jack practiced Kāloakūlua's name until it slid like squid oil off his tongue. In the evenings they replayed the day's video clips. They read all the Facebook and Twitter comments out loud. They swooned when Kāloakūlua flapped her little stubby wings. They applauded her first step. They laughed at how she built new nests and tugged playfully on low-hanging branches. They couldn't believe her friendship with a young rooster. They hollered like soccer fans when Kāloakūlua's mother chased away a few bratty albatross adolescents. When Kāloakūlua was four months old and hadn't had a meal in almost two weeks, Jack asked Lisa if she could use PayPal to send his allowance to buy squid. When they talked about it, Lisa felt grateful for how Kāloakūlua had reconnected her with her son, and how she'd finally gained some distance from her grief related to her divorce. She and Jack watched Kāloakūlua grow into a fat fuzzball and later into a big bird with beautiful feathers and long elegant wings. They wanted nothing more than the chick's well-being—until it was almost time for her to fledge.

Lisa's stomach sank just thinking about it. She wanted the young bird to fly, she really did. Sort of. No, seriously, she did. She bargained. Kāloakūlua could go, but not quite yet. Kāloakūlua could go, but not until she saw her mother Kaluahine one more time. She could go, but only if Lisa and Jack were watching the cam the moment it happened.

Lisa stared at the cards in the poker hand of her heart.

She was not ready to fold. She hedged her bets.

I see your today and raise you tomorrow.

One day Twitter announced the inevitable: Kāloakūlua had flown. It was caught on video. Lisa and Jack watched it, again and again. Jack cheered. Lisa cried. There was something so final about Kāloakūlua's launching over the open ocean, something about how the bird never looked back. Something about her detachment. About how she never said good-bye.

A few days later Lisa was standing at the sink washing dishes. Her mind was totally messing with her. Her mind told her she was foolish, that Kāloakūlua meant a lot to her, but that Lisa meant nothing to the bird. Her mind told her it was no different than her marriage. It chided her for caring so much. It ridiculed her inability to accept reality. It called her selfish.

Lisa had no rebuttal. Tears rolled down her neck. Her hands still in dishwater, she wiped her nose on her sleeve. Jack saw her.

"Awkward," he said, emphasizing the first syllable.

"What if Kāloakūlua took our happiness with her when she left?" Lisa asked, ignoring the snot on her shirt.

"I miss her too," Jack replied.

"It doesn't show," Lisa said.

"You're not telling the story right, Mom," he said. Lisa hadn't heard those words since Jack was much younger,, back when she used to read him to sleep. He used to scold her when she failed to read verbatim what was printed on the page.

"Do you want Kāloakūlua to live a long time or not?" he asked.

"Please hand me your plate," she said.

"You're not listening," he said.

"Sorry," Lisa said.

"You have to stop thinking about what you don't want, Mom. You have to start thinking about what you *do* want."

"Okay," she said.

"Whatever you think about, that's totally what you get," he said.

"You're very wise," Lisa said.

"Can we watch *Frozen* now?" Jack said.

Never before had I broken a bone. I'd spent decades working in the chaotic intimacy of hospitals, so I'd seen thousands of fractures in various phases of fixation: casted, splinted, screwed, hung from traction and bolted with complex hardware that could pick up frequencies from Finland. But none of them had been my own.

It happened when I was hiking above an isolated Kaua'i beach, camera harnessed to my back. The goal was an albatross-in-flight photo with a backdrop of the Kīlauea lighthouse. My telephoto lens felt sacred, like a polished chalice ready to be filled with red wine. The surf was roaring huge. I had to tread carefully. Over the years, more than a few mortal souls had been snatched from the tide pools below, claimed in perpetuity by winter waves. I had been out on this bluff a dozen times and knew how to stay above the water's reach. I didn't have a death wish. I had a passion for taking for shots of birds when they were being themselves rather than being suspicious of a human in the 'hood.

A small flock of ruddy turnstones fluttered onto a lava ledge not far from me, their legs as orange as a monk's robe. I crept closer for a better shot, as riveted as a raptor. I spotted a bush big enough to use as a blind. In dry conditions, ironwood seedpods are like brown ball bearings underfoot. When the soil is wet from rain and ocean spray, they're like brown ball bearings on a bed of black ice.

The last step toward my hiding place was, as they say, a doozy. My brain had zero seconds to consider my predicament. This is not a rounded-off estimate. Without a single command from my cerebral cortex, my right arm shot up precisely as fast as my Tevas lost traction, stopping my free fall with a five-fingered grip on an exposed root I had heretofore not noticed.

Crack, snapped my shoulder, irritated as all get out. I may have blurted out a syllable that roughly rhymed.

For a moment I dangled one-armed like Tarzan, in a world of pain. Somehow my feet found solid ground. The turnstones didn't budge, so completely preoccupied as they were—who could've guessed it—with turning over stones. Plus the ocean was so thundering loud I doubt they heard me. They actually looked rather stoned standing in the surf's smoky mist. My arm, on the contrary, was not what you'd call mellow. It had a very rude opinion about my little misstep.

Like any nurse, I self-triaged. I knew I didn't need immediate medical attention. I was planning to fly to Honolulu to work the next day anyway. I took a few snaps of the ruddies, then found my way back up the trail. My niece, who was enchanted with watching a tide pool farther back on the trail, never saw my fall. She drove me home.

On Oʻahu I had an appointment with an orthopedic surgeon I had known since he was a bright-eyed medical student. "That cracking sound earned you an MRI," he said. When he read the report an hour later, he smirked. "You busted it." In his declarative, "dude" was silent but implied. His jock-to-jock attitude bestowed considerably higher status on me than if I had, say, fallen down in a gutter, incontinent and drunk. (Or alternatively, if I had slipped on the freshly mopped floor at a nursing home, incontinent and drugged.)

Maya

I left the office feeling a tipsy brew of emotions: grateful that I didn't need surgery; giddy that my arm had known how to act before my conscious mind had the first clue; proud that a bone of mine was so unconditionally willing to give it up for the team; forgivably foolish (as opposed to unforgivably stupid) for the accident; vulnerable from my bumper-car bounce against the chassis of death.

The MRI acquitted me of being a wimpy hypochondriac. No, this pain had a source anyone could see. How often does a person get that luxury? It's not like the grief when your mother has still not come back to life after all these years. It's not like the despair after hearing one more awful story about how our species treats children and animals. Or like the times when the magic has ditched you so utterly you think the notion of divinity is a big fat fib fabricated by profiteers and misogynists who only want you to make a large donation to their cause.

No. There was an awe, a holy essence to that MRI. We think we're so smart with our prefrontal cortices, but I loved it that my body instinctively wanted to stay alive without asking input from "me." My arm just said "I'm going in." No rehearsals, no warm-ups, no warnings.

Plus this was a pain that would resolve. Tincture of time was its cure. The simple purity of it got me high. I fell in love with my humerus. I hugged it close and made promises about fidelity and forever, about having and holding, for better or for worse.

You may consider this our commitment announcement.

If you look closely at Maya's face, you will notice her left eye is blind. The loss of vision was likely a result of avian pox contracted from mosquitoes when she was a young chick. The insects also gave her a condition called crossbill. Her upper and lower mandibles were misaligned—rendering her bill a mediocre tool, similar to a pair of cheap tweezers. Biologists have predicted poor survival of one-eyed and crossbill fledglings because of the difficulty they would have in foraging for seafood.

Yet there she was, several years old, looking fit, visiting Kaua'i for the third year in a row. Yes, she was usually alone. Yes, she had a tendency to hang out deeper in the woods than most other birds. Yes, she joined the courtship activities on the bluff, but only briefly. I didn't know her chances for finding a mate, but they seemed pretty slim.

I named her Maya as a tribute to Maya Angelou and her seemingly bottomless reserve of courage, tenacity, and talent. I also named her in honor of the Hindu goddess of dreams and delusions, the goddess who informs us about the illusory nature of the material world. I was moved every time I saw Maya the mōlī.

Although she was the essence of perseverance and possibility, at first I called her One-Eyed Jackie. I kept that up until one day I busted myself. Why did I pick a name that focused on what she lacked rather than celebrate what she'd accomplished? In fact, why do we use a singular descriptor as a primary definition of anyone, especially those words that isolate and magnify qualities that make us the most uncomfortable? Blind, black, bipolar, gay, unwed, Republican, illegitimate, invalid (note dual pronunciations), Mormon, Muslim, retarded, rich, obese, elderly?

Not long ago a colleague of mine went missing while hiking in the mountains of Kaua'i. No trace of her was found for nearly forty-eight hours. The story made statewide headlines. Pam was a public persona, known as a nurse, a philanthropist, and an athlete. Since childhood she had explored the trails where she eventually got lost. Still, media coverage described her primarily by her chronological age, which morphed from a number to a title. She *became* seventy-two years old. She was no longer a nurse, a philanthropist, and an athlete. Friends of mine, people who didn't know her, questioned her lack of judgment, asking me why she would go walking alone in the woods. In their minds, the dominant focus of the news had molded her into only one thing: a little old lady.

When Pam was found uninjured, she revealed an entirely different picture than the superficial stereotype. She said she knew what constituted an emergency, and getting dehydrated did not qualify. She said she had not been scared. There were no bears or homicidal hikers. The temperatures were moderate. She was versed in staying warm and making herself discoverable to rescuers. Except for the fact she got lost on Mother's Day and made her family frantic, she was amused by the ordeal.

When I look more closely at Maya's photo now, her silvery blue eye looks more like a medal than a misfortune. I salute her. I salute the courageous survivor who—as it turns out—is pretty much every last one of us.

Thanks to the wisdom I found in *Motherless Daughters* by Hope Edelman, many years ago I was able to start modifying my old promise to Beatrice. I began to see my mom with more grown-up eyes, noticing the interests and choices we shared. I became more aware of the many covert ways I tried to bring her back, or at least be of service to her. When I played my comedy character, *Ivy Push, RN,* I was performing to entertain my mother. I was performing to make her more visible. When I founded a program called Bosom Buddies that offered free Healing Touch sessions, I was serving Beatrice by serving women with breast cancer. When I produced the Chuckle Channel for inpatient televisions, it was to give my hospitalized mother something uplifting to watch. When I researched humor and cancer in the Comedy in Chemotherapy (COMIC) Study, it was to measure the capacity of comedy to serve Beatrice. The list goes on.

Motherless Daughters helped me begin making the shift from "getting over" Beatrice's death. It was an astonishing relief to learn that my primary job was much simpler. My work was to *accept* her death, not fight it or deny it, and—most importantly—not take the blame for it or try to resurrect her body. With my gradual acceptance came a few memories and insights. It made me smile to imagine how it must have been for Beatrice to raise a daughter like me. Her first child, my sister, was feminine and attractive, talented in music and art. I was the second child, the one who cut off my hair with sewing scissors after I got a perm, just in time for the school photo. I was the one who drew the outline of a zipper with a black crayon on my red corduroys so they'd look like boy's pants. I was the one who refused to hold a doll or play dress-up even when everyone else in my Camp Fire troop was doing it. I was the one who was bored silly with piano lessons from Beatrice but ecstatic with my cousin Tony's hand-me-down electric train. I was the crowing hen who constantly worried Granny Ruth. Her poor missionary heart must have fibrillated every time someone looked at me asked, "Are you a boy or a girl?"

As I got closer to accepting the reality of Beatrice's death, I got closer to accepting the reality of Virg. I never did hear the word *stepmother* without an internal wince. I hope I managed to hide those winces from her. To her credit, Virg never really tried to take my mother's place. I grew to respect her, but I can't say I ever grew warm toward her. I regret that. It's not something I could force to happen. I did learn to appreciate how much my dad Chuck loved Virg, and that gave me enough fuel to make my relationship with her work.

The undertow of the commitment I made to Beatrice was still power-ful when I started monitoring albatross colonies. After a couple of sea-sons, however, I noticed subtle but vital changes in myself and wondered whether I could attribute them to the birds. Once, in a conversation with a renowned seabird biologist, I asked about Fawne's recovery from Lyme disease. The biologist nodded, describing albatross as "curative." I wouldn't have been surprised if she had said "restorative" or "healing," but suggest-ing the eradication of an illness? Yet here was a fine scientist with a doc-torate and decades of experience, a woman who understood the workings of disease. I considered the idea. Was I, like Fawne, being cured?

I retraced my mental steps. My enthusiasm for the birds had been a constant. I jumped in fast and made some errors, but not once in eleven years had I gotten bored, nor did I ever think I knew everything I needed to know. In the company of albatross I felt kinship and content-ment, which would have been enough. More than enough. There was also a gradual decrease in my negative mental chatter; more accurately, it began to have less volume.

There was no question I had committed myself to the birds, to my 'aumākua. I knew that service itself—not any specific outcome—was the taproot to the truth. If I was serving my ancestors, I was serving

Beatrice. If I was paddling in the right direction, it mattered less if I had doubts about my competence or my stamina.

I also began to untie myself from the knots of my own possessive urges. As far back as I can remember, I wanted to touch birds, to feel their soft feathers, to imagine they cared about me as I cared about them. I was drawn to the fantasy of being one of the few humans they trusted, a veritable Nurse Doolittle. The birds were healing me of those notions. It took time for me to realize possessiveness was just another form of colonialism and a means of subjugating others for personal gain. If I reached out and touched a bird, whom would I be serving? I would only be causing distress to a creature I claimed to adore.

Once I accepted I would never "know" the albatross in that way, it was easier to gaze at them, not unlike the way I gaze at stars. To watch them, not unlike the way I watch whales. To admire their beauty, not unlike the way I admire rainbows. To separate them—as much as humanly possible—from my personal needs and projections.

We may never know why Makani the Wayfinder was drawn to Kauaʻi in the late seventies. Some people consider it a miracle; others see it as a mistake. Some see it as a prophetic warning about rising sea levels and the ultimate submersion of her mother ship at Midway. Some say Makani was sent by unseen forces so she could find a Noah's ark for her species. Some say Makani was merely following a biological urge and quite coincidentally landed on a populated island. Any and all of those explanations could be true. In the end, the fact that she started a new colony on Kauaʻi matters more to me than theories about what brought her there.

Like Makani, I may never know why I was suddenly so drawn to Kauaʻi in the late seventies. It would have been easy to forget about my dream visitation by Martha Beckwith. It would have been easy to ignore the concept of ʻaumākua and to miss the living presence of my ancestors. It would have been easy to be too preoccupied or intimidated to become an albatross advocate. I now see each of those decisive moments as my own personal acts of fledging, as leaps of faith from one stage to the next, of finding my way without knowing my way, and of obeying that which guides me.

Vertical flight

Albatross also follow their noses. For one thing, they can smell food from several miles away. But mōlī tubenoses come equipped with another cool function: inside their nostrils is a speedometer. It informs the birds when they're moving at just the right speed to bank steeply and fly vertically, their wings perpendicular to the earth, for just a moment, without losing lift, in order to change direction without a single wingbeat, loving the ride, trusting they will stay aloft, their heads held horizontally and their eyes focused on where the wind and gravity are taking them.

What other internal instruments guide them? Perhaps the willingness of mōlī to share close proximity with humans doesn't mean what we'd like to think. Perhaps we simply haven't registered on their radar yet. They've had millions of years to work out their survival strategies, and our species is still very young on the planet. When that bird stepped on my foot all those years ago, maybe she was living in a different era, long before people existed. Maybe she inadvertently gave me a peek through a peephole into an ancient time, into deep time. Who can say?

I know one thing for sure about albatross: they are always completely themselves. In such purity there is raw perfection. When I can feel that perfection, I can see glimpses of perfection in myself and others. The kind of perfection that is the birthright of all of us. The kind of perfection we feel best in the company of newborns and baby animals. The kind of perfection that makes us know we belong. The kind of perfection that allows room for everyone else.

What better way to live?

My life contains all the generations before me. I am Clarissa the strong and Makani the Wayfinder. I am Luka the navigator. I am Martha the scribe. I am Granny Ruth, coldcocked by grief. I am Hōkūlani and I am Lolana, a partner in long-lasting love. I am Toodles, stabbing hearts with sharp words. I am Mango, launching from infinity. I am Annette the generous. I am Caroline, trapped in the belly of my mother's illness. I am Makai, my child stolen. I am Randy the prayer and Townie the answer. I am an admirer of the royal families and traditional cultures of Hawai'i and Bhutan. I am Juana Cota and Jose Manuel, chanting the ancient wisdom of my clan. I am Virg, innocently stumbling into an impossible job. I am Large Marge and Plenny Lenny, finding the fun in the storm. I am Kaluahine, growing up. I am Ola and Loa, missing my mother unto death. I am Trudy and I am Frau Krankyhosen, creating rules to protect me from my own fears. I am a dog-bit chick, losing everything I know. I am The Librarian, confused by split loyalties. I am Macaroon, dying. I am Paki, living in a stranger's home. I am Onipa'a, discovering friends in surprising places. I am Lisa, learning from my own child. I am Maya, an intrepid survivor. I am Fawne, cured. I am Gracie, finding new love in old places. I am Kāloakūlua, inheriting strength from my ancestors. I am Chuck, going with the flow.

I am Beatrice, alive in the stories of birds.

Acknowledgments

When I began making a list of people who helped make *Holy Mōlī* possible, I thought it would take a few hours to complete. But such freely given support has been offered to me over the years, I discovered a much larger opportunity for appreciation. Every name below represents a significant contribution of encouragement, editing, mentoring, criticism, collegiality, and/or insight. There isn't enough space to include details on every individual, but I trust each of them will know why they matter so much.

Mahalo for the friendship of Carl Safina and Pat Paladines as well as the great honor of being named a Safina Center Fellow 2016–2017. Mahalo to Beth Flint, for teaching me about mōlī fieldwork and for suggesting the creation of the Kaua'i Albatross Network (KAN). To biologists Aaron Hebshi and Lindsay Young for answering my never-ending questions. Gratitude to the amazing KAN team, including Hōkū Cody, Susan Dierker, Delores Gourley, John Harter, Marcia Harter, Mika Ashley-Hollinger, Stuart Hollinger, Makaala Kaaumoana, Baba Siri Singh Khalsa, Barb Mayer, Jeanine Meyers, Kevin Meyers, Nicki Pignoli, Jody Platt, Kim Steutermann Rogers, Angie Serota, Arnie Serota, Louise Steenblik, Rick Steenblik, David Stern, Jane Stern, Robin Torquati, Grace Uilani Ventura, and Paul Ventura.

Many thanks to the Cornell Lab of Ornithology, especially Miyoko Chu, Charles Eldermire, Hugh Powell, and Hollie Sutherland, not to mention all the fabulous women who selflessly volunteered for thousands of hours of TrossCam duties.

A standing ovation for Jessica Weber, Sara Levins, Sy Montgomery, Leslie Meredith, Sarah Jane Freymann, and Jennie Chin Hansen for playing such extraordinary and well-choreographed roles in a mysterious virtual musical on the streets of NYC. I will never forget your welcoming or your willingness.

With great respect to Her Royal Majesty Ashi Dorji Wangmo Wangchuck, for kindly agreeing to be interviewed by an unknown American, and to my *hānai* family Karma Tsering, Jigme Tsering, and Tshering Pem, each of whom taught me more about Bhutan than I dreamed possible.

To Pono Shim, Sam Ohu Gon III, Sabra Kauka, Puanani Burgess, Mahealani Wendt, and Hōkū Cody with gratitude for your blessings and Hawaiian cultural insights.

To Brian Doyle and David James Duncan—my spiritual littermates —for writing your hearts out, for making me laugh no matter what, and for astonishing me with the power of words to infuse our dreams with love. To all the other stellar faculty of the annual Hanalei Writers' Retreat, each of whom has taught the craft of rigorous writing: Terry Tempest Williams, Kim Stafford, Kathleen Dean Moore, Hope Edelman, Gina Barreca, Carl Safina, and Cheryl Strayed. Mahalo too for the steadfast support of Carol Wilcox, Susan O'Connor, Maile Meyer, and Takiora Ingram. Special gratitude to all the retreat attendees, whose comments helped give *Holy Mōlī* structure and essence.

To Vaden Y.F.W. Riggs, my beloved high school English teacher, for daring to give an F to a sixteen-year-old for a lazy essay. To Nick Despota, for many skills and open-hearted generosity.

More thanks to believers and bird fans, stretching from this morning to long ago—including Jim Allen, Lisa Anselme, Adrian Arleo, Edward Armbrecht, C. J. Artinyan, Mickey Babcock, Claudia Bachman, Ken Bachman, Sherry Beckett, Talia Beebe, Thomas Beebe, Coleen Belisle, Leinaala Benson, Jackie Bernard, Marge Bernice, Chuck Betlach, Connie Black, Heather Anne Bolen, Mimsy Bouret, Gary Braasch, Marcella "Sparkle Plenty" Brady, Sharon Britt, Bonnie Bruckheimer, Marcia Brumbaugh, Nancy Budd, Judy Burner, Jean Cantu, Stephanie Castillo, Dana Davis Childs, Patrick Ching, Shambhavi Christian, Myra Christopher, Hollis Church, Janie Coltrin, Dan Cooney, Nancy Cowan, Carol Curtiss, Joan Cvengros, Rosalie Danbury, Susan Davis, Anne Day, Larry Day, Ellen Weigant Dishman, Teal Doggett, Mary Miller Doyle, Anne Earhart, Lois Ann Ell, Clarissa Emayo, Bea Enright, Rory Enright, Dick Ferguson, Jean Ferguson, Rick Ferguson, Kshama Ferrar,

Tina Ferrato, Betty Ferrell, Joanna Fielder, Judith Flanders, Noni Floyd, Petty Floyd, Niranjani Forest, Candy Fowler, Greg Fowler, Fawne Frailey, Danny Galas, Robin Galas, Jennifer Gaskin, Val Gebert, Darien Gee, Deborah Gillikin, Carrol Godwin, Cody Godwin, Bud Greer, Judi Greer, Juliana Grigorova, Dahlia Griffin, Zoe Griffin, Amy Gulick, Keren Gunderson, Betty Gurany, Constance Hale, Panna Hamilton, Joseph Hanwright, Patricia Hanwright, Carol Harding, Marietta Mears Haskell, Bob Hobdy, Doreen Tasha Hobdy, Jane Hoffman, Frances Imamura, Peter Jaret, David John, Makaala Kaaumoana, Nalani Kaneakua, Kawehionalani Kauhola, Jim Kennedy, Shawn Kennedy, Vickie Kennedy, Jason Kimura, David Kingston, Leah Kliger, Susan Kobayashi, Beth Ann Kozlovich, Swami Kripananda, Savitri Kumaran, Audrey Kumasaka, Giles Larrain, Louda Larrain, Sherilyn Lee, Joan Leitzer, Sara Levins, Jennifer Luck, Marilyn Mach, Tess Marino, Aggie Marti-Kini, Leo McCarthy, Mary McManus, Ernestine Melton, Louise Mita, Patty Mittendorff, Stella Moon, Matt Morelock, Heather Murch, Glen Nishida, Stephan Nobs, Nancy Norton, D'Arcy Nunn, Stacey O'Brien, Gary Okamoto, Polli Oliver, Anne O'Malley, Annis Parker, Julia Parish, Bill Parrish, Catherine Parrish, Chris Pasero, Mary Paterson, Lisa Perkins, Lesley Pierce, Joan Porter, Sara Porter, Lori Protzman, Katherine Puckett, Lisa Robertson, Steve Robertson, Judy Rodrigues, Lenny Rodrigues, Mary Hill Rojas, Debbie Bird Rose, Sharon Rothschild, Gae Rusk, George Russell, Sharman Apt Russell, Ed Sancious, Phil Sandifer, Mercedes Santos, Chiz Schultz, David Scott, Susan Scott, Yasuko Shiraishi, Barbara Sloan, Barbara Lee Souder, Catherine Steinmann, Bonnie Stowe, Virginia Stowe, Angela Sun, Nancy Symington, Toby Symington, Graham Taylor, Jonna Tamases, Jeff Tamkin, Julie Tamkin, Jean Taran, Terry White Tate, Madeline Tefft, Diana Thomas, Felice Tolentino, Lorilani Keohokalole-Torio, Frank Turonis, Rich Wacker, Maile Walters, Stephanie Warburg, Jennifer Ward, Linda Ward, Anuenue Washburn, John Wehrheim, Scott Weidensaul, Marion Werner, Geoffry White, Joan White, Perry White, Rachael Wong, Pam Woolway, Patty Wooten, Susan Bauer Wu, Lara Yamada, Cammie Yee, Carol Yotsuda, JoAnn Yukimura, and Coco Zingaro.

My greatest respect and gratitude for the many conservation professionals, animal lovers, and citizen scientists who have done so much for Kaua'i native birds, including—but not remotely limited to—Don Beattie, Kathy Beattie, Ann Bell, Jessi Hallman Behnke, Beryl Blaich, John Burger, Don Brockmeier, Suzanne Case, Penny Cistaro, Dan Clark, Michelle Clark, Hōkū Cody, Andy Collins, Cali Crampton, Jim Denny, Joyce Doty, Pete Dunne, Fern Duvall, Linda Elliott, Luke Evslin, Chris Farmer, Marty Fernandes, Beth Flint, Sam Ohu Gon III, Cathy Granholm, Keren Gundersen, Margaret Hanson, Jamie Harris, Aaron Hebshi, Shannon Hibberd, Julie Hill, Peter Hodum, Becky Hommon, Ann Humphrey, Helen James, Jack Jeffrey, Makaala Kaaumoana, Thomas Kaiakapu, Jody Kaulukukui, Lizabeth Kashinsky, Marilou Knight, Bongo Lee, Chris Lepczyk, Bill Lucey, Jean Luck, Jean Olbert, Peggy Ostrom, John Peschon, Katie Pickett, Sheldon Plentovitch, Andre Raine, Pua Raines, Kathy Richardson, Kim Steutermann Rogers, Sheri Saari, Tom Savre, Bob Schleck, Sue Schubel, Robert Shallenberger, Patsy Sheehan, Jason Shimauchi, Peter Silva, Grant Sizemore, Tom Southwick, Kim Uyehara, Stacy VanderPol, Eric VanderWerf, Jennifer Waipa, George Wallace, Chipper Wichman, Kawika Winter, Arleone Dibben Young, Lindsay Young, Nate Yeun, Brenda Zaun, and Marjorie Ziegler.

To the astounding people at The Queen's Medical Center for supporting me to fledge from serving patients to serving mōlī: Suzanne Beauvallet, Francisco Conde, Daniel Fischberg, Beth Freitas, Della Graham, Mimi Harris, Jim Hubbard, Jean Imler, Cindy Kamikawa, Lydia Kumasaka, Jill Kurasaki, Shari Kogan, Joan Maeshiro, Joyce Masuda, Lynn Muneno, Lam Nguyen, Stacy Terashita, Monika Tomita, Art Ushijima, Mark Yamakawa, Claire Yoshida, and all the stupendous Healing Touch volunteers.

Finally, to Gurumayi Chidvilasananda for teachings to last lifetimes. To Tom Booth, Micki Reaman, and Marty Brown at Oregon State University Press, each of whom believed in *Holy Mōlī* from the first read, and who patiently ushered it through every instar. Most of all, to the beloved souls on Kaua'i without whom I would surely have perished a thousand times over: Jackie Barnard; Kashmir "Marmji" Gellatly; Judy Jordan; the Fun Family—AKA Kevin, Jeanine, and Mojito Meyers; Liz Thompson; my Personal Genius Bar—AKA Pammy Vincent; Eric Whitney; and to my partner Joanne Little, the wisest and most generous believer of them all.

Glossary

'āina   land, earth

akamai   smart, clever, expert

akiaki   seashore rush grass (*Sporobolus virginicus*), a coarse grass growing on sandy beaches

aloha   love, affection, compassion, mercy, sympathy, pity, kindness, sentiment, grace, charity; greeting, salutation, regards; sweetheart, lover, loved one; beloved, loving, kind, compassionate, charitable, lovable; to love, be fond of; to show kindness, mercy, pity, charity, affection; to venerate; to remember with affection; to greet, hail; Greetings! Hello! Good-by! Farewell! Alas!

'aumākua   family or personal gods, deified ancestors who may assume the shape of animals

'elepaio   species of flycatcher with subspecies on Hawai'i (*Chasiempis sandwichensis sandwichensis*), Kaua'i (*C. sandwichensis sclateri*), and O'ahu (*C. sandwichensis gayi*); believed to be the goddess of canoe makers; *'Elepaio Journal* is also the name of the Hawai'i Audubon Society Newsletter

Halele'a   moku (district) of Kaua'i

hana hou   to do again, repeat, renew, repair, mend; encore

hānai	foster child, adopted child; to foster, adopt
Hōkūlani	heavenly star; from *hōkū* "star" and *lani* "heaven, sky, royal, majesty"; in *Holy Mōlī*, an albatross character who is the daughter of Luka and Lopaka, mates with Lolana, mother of Kaluahine, and is suggested to be in the lineage of Makani
'iwa	frigate or man-of-war bird (*Fregata minor palmerstoni*); thief, so called because the 'iwa steals food by forcing other birds to disgorge
Kāloakūlua	a phase of the moon; in *Holy Mōlī* is an albatross character who is the star of Season One of Cornell Lab of Ornithology's TrossCam and is suggested to be in the lineage of Makani
Kaluahine	in *Holy Mōlī*, a female bird who nests in a specific area on Kaua'i; her mothers are Hōkūlani and Lolana; her mate is Kaluakane, and her daughter is Kāloakūlua, the star of the Cornell TrossCam Season One; suggested to be in the lineage of Makani
Kaluakane	in *Holy Mōlī*, a male bird who nests in a specific area on Kaua'i; his mate is Kaluahine and he is the father of Kāloakūlua, the star of the Cornell TrossCam Season One
Ko'olau	a moku (district) of Kaua'i; a famous Hawaiian man in Kaua'i history; in *Holy Mōlī*, the mate of Malumalu and the father of Mango
Lolana	to soar; in *Holy Mōlī* an albatross character who is the mate of Hōkūlani and mother of Kaluahine
Lopaka	Hawaiian name for Robert; in *Holy Mōlī*, an albatross character who is the mate of Luka and the father of Hōkūlani

Luka	Hawaiian name for Luca (bringer of light); in *Holy Mōlī*, an albatross character who is the first chick to fledge from Kauaʻi in perhaps a thousand years or more; is suggested to be the daughter of Makani
mahalo ke Akua	gratitude to God
mahalo na ʻaumakua	gratitude to the family or personal gods, deified ancestors who might assume the shape of animals
makai	toward the ocean; in *Holy Mōlī*, Makai is an albatross character who nests at Pacific Missile Range Facility and whose egg is taken from him in order to discourage bird-aircraft strikes
makakilo	*maka* eyes, *kilo* stargazer, seer, astrologer; to watch closely, spy, examine, look around, observe, forecast; in *Holy Mōlī*, Makakilo is a blue-eyed homeless dog who appears at Kāloakūlua's side, as seen by the Cornell Lab TrossCam, but who miraculously does not injure the chick
makani	wind, breeze; in *Holy Mōlī*, the first albatross known to raise a chick to successfully fledge from Kauaʻi in perhaps a thousand years or more; mother of Luka, the first chick to fledge from Kauaʻi in that same time period; also called Makani the Wayfinder
malama pono	take good care, be careful, watch out
malumalu	shelter or protection of any kind, often humble; shady; in *Holy Mōlī*, an albatross character who is the mate of Koʻolau and mother of Mango
mauka	toward the mountains
moku	district

mōlī	Laysan albatross (*Diomedea immutabilis*)
ola loa	long life, completely cured or recovered; in *Holy Mōlī*, Ola and Loa are albatross "twins" who hatch against impossible odds
onipa'a	fixed, immovable, motionless, steadfast, established, firm, resolute, determined; the motto of Kamehameha V and Lili'uokalani; in *Holy Mōlī*, an albatross character who befriends an old umbrella
Paki	Hawaiian for name Paddy or Patty; in *Holy Mōlī*, an albatross chick who is taken from her birth parent and given to an adoptive parent
Pihemanu	loud din of birds; Hawaiian name for Midway Atoll in the Northwestern Hawaiian Islands
pono	goodness, uprightness, morality, moral qualities, correct or proper procedure, excellence, well-being, prosperity, welfare, benefit, behalf, equity, sake, true condition or nature, duty; moral, fitting, proper, righteous, right, upright, just, virtuous, fair, beneficial, successful, in perfect order, accurate, correct, eased, relieved
tita	a strong, independent woman with a soft heart (Pidgin)

Source: *Nā Puke Wehewehe 'Ōlelo Hawai'i*, Hawaiian Electronic Dictionary, wehewehe.org

Resources

Books

Beckwith, Martha Warren. *The Kumulipo: A Hawaiian Creation Chant.* University of Chicago, 1951.

Beckwith, Martha Warren. *Hawaiian Mythology.* Yale University Press, 1940.

Dierker, Susan. *Albatross of Kaua'i: The Story of Kaloakulua.* Done by Dogs Publishing, 2014.

Pattison, Darcy. *Wisdom, the Midway Albatross: Surviving the Japanese Tsunami and Other Disasters for over 60 Years.* Mims House, 2012.

Pukui, Mary Kawena. *'Olelo No 'Eau: Hawaiian Proverbs & Poetical Sayings.* Bishop Museum Press, 1983.

Pukui, Mary Kawena. *Place Names of Hawai'i.* University of Hawa'i Press, 1974.

Roy, Tui, and Mark Jones. *Albatross: Their World, Their Ways.* Firefly Books, 2008.

Safina, Carl. *Beyond Words: What Animals Think and Feel.* Holt & Company, 2015.

Safina, Carl. *Eye of the Albatross: Visions of Hope and Survival.* Holt Paperbacks, 2003.

Strycker, Noah. *The Thing With Feathers: The Surprising Lives of Birds and What They Reveal About Being Human.* Riverhead Books, 2014.

Websites

American Bird Conservancy
abcbirds.org

Cornell Lab of Ornithology
allaboutbirds.org

Hawaiian Islands Land Trust
hilt.org

Kauaʻi Albatross Network
albatrosskauai.org

The Safina Center
safinacenter.org

The author at Midway Atoll

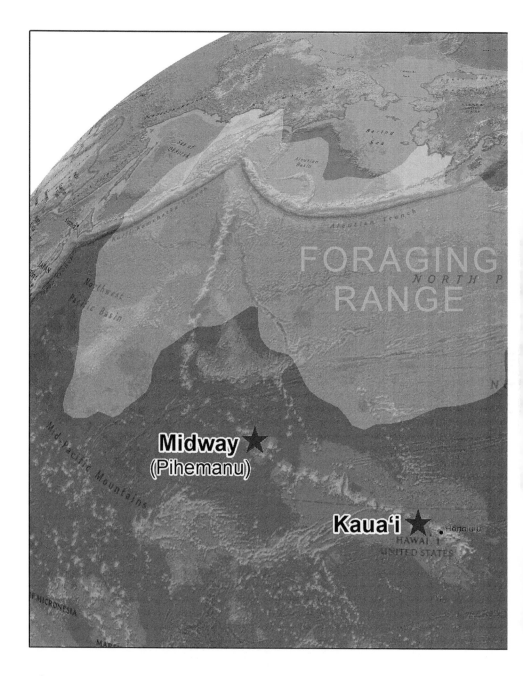

Laysan Albatross Foraging Range, Non-Nesting Season

map courtesy of The Nature Conservancy